AWAKENING TO GOD

in Everyday Life

A BIBLE STUDY BY

MELISSA SPOELSTRA

Abingdon Women | Nashville

Acts
Awakening to God in Everyday Life

Contents

About the Author

Melissa Spoelstra is a popular women's conference speaker (including the Aspire Tour), Bible teacher, and author who is madly in love with Jesus and passionate about studying God's Word and helping women of all ages to seek Christ and know Him more intimately through serious Bible study. Having a degree in Bible theology, she enjoys teaching God's Word to the body of Christ and traveling to diverse groups and churches across the nation and also to Nairobi, Kenya, for a women's prayer conference. Melissa is the author of the Bible studies *The Names of God: His Character Revealed*, *Romans: Good News That Changes Everything*, *Elijah: Spiritual Stamina in Every Season*, *Numbers: Learning Contentment in a Culture of More*, *First Corinthians: Living Love When We Disagree*, *Joseph: The Journey to Forgiveness*, and *Jeremiah: Daring to Hope in an Unstable World*, and the books *Dare to Hope: Living Intentionally in an Unstable World*, *Total Family Makeover: 8 Practical Steps to Making Disciples at Home*, and *Total Christmas Makeover: 31 Devotions to Celebrate with Purpose*. She is a regular contributor to the Proverbs 31 First Five App and the Girlfriends in God online daily devotional. She has published articles in *ParentLife*, *Women's Spectrum*, and *Just Between Us* and writes her own regular blog in which she shares her musings about what God is teaching her on any given day. Melissa lives in Pickerington, Ohio, with her pastor husband, Sean, and their four kids: Zach, Abby, Sara, and Rachel.

Follow Melissa:

 @MelSpoelstra

 @Daring2Hope

 @Author MelissaSpoelstra

Her blog   MelissaSpoelstra.com
(check here also for event dates and booking information)

Introduction to this Study

The word *awakening* makes me think of mornings, and I've never been accused of being a morning person. My alarm jolts me awake on weekdays, and immediately the mental bargaining begins as I consider reasons to hit snooze. Even though I love sleep, awakening is essential to living life. When I wake up, I experience sights and sounds that I wasn't conscious of while asleep. I have full awareness of myself and my surroundings.

Just as we awaken physically each day, so we must awaken spiritually in our everyday lives. By this I mean opening our spiritual eyes and ears to experience the power and presence of God with a fresh perspective. Often, I find myself drifting toward spiritual detachment, failing to notice God's Spirit at work within and around me. The Lord is always working, but sometimes I become "spiritually sleepy," such as when attachments to things of the world—social media, television, material possessions, and physical pleasures—deaden my senses to God's Spirit; disciplines such as prayer, Bible study, worship, journaling, silence, and other spiritual rhythms become rote (or neglected); my tasks become more important than relationships with God and people; or seasons of grief or difficulty persist, or things go relatively well for a long time, resulting in my tendency to coast or slide into spiritual apathy.

These are just some of the scenarios that reveal a need for spiritual awakening in my life. Other times I get in a rut and have no idea why I feel like I'm spiritually sleepwalking through my day. Whether or not you have a case of the blahs today, perhaps you can relate to the spiritual sleepiness or drift toward indifference we all experience at times. Just as being awake physically involves awareness, being awake spiritually involves becoming more and more aware of where and how God is already working in our lives.

As we study the Book of Acts, we'll be exploring our ongoing need for this spiritual awareness as we witness God's Spirit birth and grow the early church by awakening them to His power, message, freedom, grace, mission, and direction. Sometimes God's Spirit jolted the people awake like an alarm clock, and other times He moved them with a gentle call. From their experiences we will learn some postures that will help us to attune our own spiritual hearts to experience God's presence, hear God's voice, and see God's Spirit at work.

God used ordinary men and women like you and me in extraordinary ways to spread His message of grace demonstrated through the sacrifice of His Son. It was necessary for the early church to awaken to God in order to accomplish this vital mission, and the same is true for us. We must break free of spiritual sleepiness and awaken to God's Spirit in everyday life if we are to accomplish the mission of sharing Jesus's message today.

The apostle Paul said in Acts 20:24, "But my life is worth nothing to me unless I use it for finishing the work assigned me by the Lord Jesus—the work of telling others the Good News about the wonderful grace of God." We have been entrusted with this same message for our generation. So we must fight against slipping into apathy, where we see only human realities, and ask God to awaken us to His supernatural possibilities.

This posture isn't usually the path of least resistance. The early church faced many trials. They had relationship and leadership problems within their own church bodies. From the very beginning of the church, there were all manner of arguments. Church has always been messy! The early church also felt pressure from the world around them. The government, idol worshippers, and even Jewish leaders oppressed them in their organizational infancy. Yet despite all of these difficulties, the church prevailed through an ongoing awakening to God's Spirit. If their passion for God could be reignited, so can ours.

As Christ-followers, we need a fresh encounter with God so that we are drawn deeper into God's love, prepared for daily battles, and made ready to share God's love with others. Through the pages of Acts, we get a glimpse into a divinely empowered movement that changed the world. I am so excited to turn those pages alongside you and experience an awakening to God in our everyday lives!

About the Study

As we unpack the Book of Acts one chapter at a time, we will find ourselves journeying with the early followers of Jesus as they respond to God's Spirit in their everyday lives. Here's a brief overview:

Week 1: In the first four chapters, the early believers awaken to God's power as the Holy Spirit makes a grand appearance on the day of Pentecost. We will focus on the powerlessness we feel in our faith and realign ourselves to the power God offers us through His Word, His promises, His Spirit, His name, and prayer.

Week 2: In chapters 5–9, we'll find an emphasis on awakening to God's message of love and grace even in the face of those who defame or dilute the true gospel. We will gain confidence and clarity about what it means to be a Christ-follower and how we can share God's gospel message.

Week 3: The next five chapters, 10–14, highlight God's church awakening to freedom in Christ. We all have seasons when we slip into the bondage of either legalism or license and need to awaken afresh to the freedom God longs to give us in Christ.

Week 4: In chapters 15–19, we find that God invites His church to keep an open mind like the Bereans had and to exercise discernment with the many messages coming our way. We also want to keep our hearts and minds open to how God invites us into relationship with Him today.

Week 5: Chapters 20–24 center around the apostle Paul's missionary journeys and remind us that we too have been commissioned to share God's love with others. We want the world to know about Jesus, and we will take some time to consider how the Lord awakens us personally to bloom right where He has planted us.

Week 6: We'll finish the Book of Acts by awakening to God's direction in chapters 25–28, realizing that His plans often look different from ours. If you have questions for the Lord about what comes next in your life, we'll find the last chapters in Acts relevant as we seek God's direction personally.

Throughout our study, we will look for God's initiatives and the early church's responses. Every lesson ends with a section called Daily Wrap-Up, where we will reflect on the same two questions each day:

- What is one way you noticed God at work in the chapter?
- How did the believers respond?

Some days God's work will be easily identifiable, such as when we read about healings, miracles, or other divine interventions. Other times, we will find the Lord working behind the scenes, such as when He is leading people, allowing difficult circumstances, or encouraging community.

The ladies who piloted this study found that the two Daily Wrap-Up questions were occasionally challenging to answer. After discussing it, we decided that taking the time to reflect on God's work at each juncture of the story in Acts is a worthy pursuit. If you struggle from time to time with the Daily Wrap-Up, know that you are in good company. Wrestling and questioning is a practice that brings growth, and I invite you to embrace the process. Though I offer some thoughts of my own following the questions, there are no definitive answers here, and I encourage you to share your own thoughts and ideas.

In this process, we'll learn together from the early believers what postures and practices led them to awaken to God in their everyday lives so that we might be inspired to follow their example. Their gathering, praying, fasting, traveling, studying, sharing, organizing, obeying, and learning through both success and failure will challenge us to ask God to awaken our hearts to Him in a way that impacts our thoughts and behaviors.

The Daily Wrap-Up ends with a review of the Big Idea for the day and a question regarding your key takeaway from the lesson. We don't just want to observe the action in Acts; we want to awaken to the action of God in our own lives. This will require times of stillness and listening as we reflect on God's movement in the early church and seek greater awareness of Him in our everyday lives. My prayer is that we would end our study not only completing the activities in this workbook but also truly awakening to God's Spirit as we seek Him together.

Options for Study

Before beginning the study, I invite you to consider the level of commitment your time and life circumstances will allow. I have found that what I put into a Bible study directly correlates to what I get out of it. When I commit to do the homework daily, God's truths sink deeper as I take time to reflect and meditate on what God is teaching me. When I am intentional about gathering with other women in person or online to watch videos and have discussion, I find that this helps keep me from falling off the Bible study wagon midway. Also, making a point to memorize verses and dig deeper by looking at additional materials greatly benefits my soul.

At other times, however, I have bitten off more than I can chew. When our faith is new, our children are small, or there are great demands on our time because of difficult circumstances or challenges, we need to be realistic about what we will be able to finish. This study is designed with options that enable you to tailor it to your particular circumstances and needs.

1. Basic Study. The basic study includes five daily readings or lessons. Each lesson combines study of Scripture with personal reflection and application (boldface type indicates write-in-the-book questions and activities), ending with a Daily Wrap-Up, a Talk with God sample prayer, and a Big Idea, or takeaway, from the lesson. On average, you will need about twenty to thirty minutes to complete each lesson.

At the end of each week, you will find a Weekly Wrap-Up to guide you in a quick review of what you've learned. You don't want to skip this part, which you'll find to be one of the most practical tools of the study. This brief exercise will help your takeaways from the lessons to "stick," making a real and practical difference in your daily life.

When you gather with your group to review each week's material, you will watch a video, discuss what you are learning, and pray together. I encourage you to discuss the insights you are gaining and how God is working in your own life.

2. Deeper Study. If you want an even deeper study, there are memory verses for each week, and you'll find a memorization exercise at the end of each lesson.

3. Lighter Commitment. If you are in a season of life in which you need a lighter commitment, I encourage you to give yourself permission to do what you can. God will bless your efforts and speak to you through this study at every level of participation.

Take time now to pray and decide which study option is right for you, and check it below.

1. __ Basic Study
2. __ Deeper Study
3. __ Lighter Commitment: I will_____.

Be sure to let someone in your group know which option you have chosen to do so that you have some accountability and encouragement.

A Final Word

Awakening to God's Spirit not only birthed the church but also sustains it today. We can respond to the Holy Spirit as the body of Christ in this generation and experience God's power, message, freedom, grace, mission, and direction. Whether we are currently experiencing divine energy or wanting to push the snooze button on God's spiritual alarm clock a few more times, studying the Book of Acts will awaken us to God in fresh ways. Let's focus on the journey ahead and ask the Lord to awaken us to His Spirit today and every day!

Melissa

Video Viewer Guide:
Introductory Video (Optional)

Just as we awaken _____, we can also awaken _____.

Attachments to things of the world like _____ _____, _____,
_____ _____, and physical pleasures deaden my senses to
God's Spirit at work within and around me.

Disciplines such as _____, _____ _____, _____,
_____, _____ and other spiritual rhythms become rote (or
neglected).

My _____ become more important than _____ God and people.

Acts 20:24

"But my life is worth nothing to me unless I use it for finishing the work assigned me by
the Lord Jesus—the work of _____ _____ _____ _____ _____
_____ _____ _____ _____ ____ _____."

Awakening to God's Spirit not only _____ the church, but also _____ it
today.

Week 1

Awakening to God's Power

Acts 1–4

Memory Verse

"But you will receive power when the Holy Spirit comes upon you. And you will be my witnesses, telling people about me everywhere—in Jerusalem, throughout Judea, in Samaria, and to the ends of the earth."

(Acts 1:8)

Day 1: The Power of the Pen

My favorite novels chronicle two stories intermittently. They begin with one story line from the past and then introduce a different thread that includes modern characters. The author alternates chapters while developing both narratives. These story lines eventually intertwine as events that occurred in the past impact the present.

As we embark on a study of Acts, I pray that each day finds us in two stories where the narrative of the people of the early church intersects with the story of each of our lives. We will unpack this account of the birth of the church, traditionally believed to be written by a man named Luke, and meet men and women who lived centuries ago.

The posture we take toward our study will be key in determining our receptivity to awakening to God's power.

Take a moment to consider the adjectives below, and circle any that describe your current spiritual position:

Curious	Apathetic	Tentative	Weary	Eager
Distant	Hungry	Dry	Engaged	Agitated
Stagnant	Flourishing	Growing	Other_____	

You might have circled two words that seem opposite, because many times we feel conflicted in our spiritual life. I will admit that a study of Acts greatly appeals to me because I have felt spiritually stagnant in recent months. I long for an awakening to more of God's power and presence in my life. How about you? As you reflect on your life, I hope the thought of awakening to a greater awareness of God appeals to you too.

What are one or two differences you would like to see in your spiritual life by the end of our study?

I hope that my desire to spread God's message of love will be reignited and that the Holy Spirit will grow my faith as I remember God is always speaking. I like how one commentator referred to Acts as a dialogue between a "God who refuses to be silent and a community that tries to listen."[2] It is my prayer that a renewed passion for active listening will be a key outcome of our study for all of us. The Book of Acts is so much more than a historical record of the

Big Idea

We can awaken to God's power because He has given us His Word.

Extra Insight

In the late second century, the early church father Irenaeus referred to the book as the Acts of the Apostles. One commentator said that a more accurate title would be Acts of the Holy Spirit.[1]

Theologians
debate the genre
and purpose
of Acts, but the
majority describe
the book with the
word *kerygma*,
which means
"proclamation."
The Book of Acts
proclaims the
works of God using
historical narrative.[3]

church's beginnings. We want our study of Acts to permeate our lives as we listen carefully to the inspired words of God's Spirit.

We will cover one chapter of Acts each day, but before we dig into the text, I believe some background information on the author will enhance our reading of God's Word. Some of you are sharpening your pencils while others of you are inwardly groaning. If you are in the latter group, hang in there because understanding this background will prove helpful before we immerse ourselves in twenty-eight chapters covering approximately thirty years that changed the world!

According to church tradition, Acts was written by a man named Luke (author of the Gospel of Luke) under the inspiration of the Holy Spirit. Before we open his manuscript, we are going to get to know the author himself. Knowing the person on the other side of the pen can enhance our understanding of what we are reading.

Who are some of your favorite authors and why? What have you enjoyed learning about them, or what would you like to know about them?

Perhaps you have enjoyed learning the background of a nonfiction author who challenges your thinking, or perhaps you would like to know the influences of a novelist who draws you into the story. I have enjoyed learning that Jane Austen first published my favorite novel, *Pride and Prejudice*, anonymously because women weren't allowed to have any other roles than wife and mother in society. Her name never appeared on any of her books during her lifetime. Just as it can be helpful to learn about our favorite authors, knowing about a biblical author can give us great insight into the text.

Are there things you already know about the author Luke? If so, write them below:

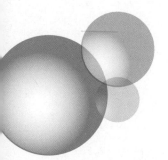

If you didn't write anything, that's okay! Here are four key facts about Luke that enrich our study of Acts. He was:

- **an investigator** (who listened to firsthand accounts and compiled and condensed information),
- **a Gentile** (which provided him a unique perspective from the other New Testament writers, who were of Jewish heritage),

- **an educated doctor** (who humbly elevated others' stories rather than his own), and
- **a ministry partner of Paul** (with firsthand knowledge of many of the events recorded in Acts).

Luke was not one of Jesus's twelve disciples, so he relied on eyewitnesses and investigation as he prepared his account—which originally was written as a two-volume work[4] and later was separated into Luke and Acts (when the four Gospels were ordered according to when they were thought to have been written). In a sense, we might say that the Gospel of Luke serves as an introduction to Acts.

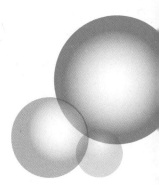

Read Luke 1:1-4 and answer the following questions:

What did people use as sources to write accounts of Jesus and the early church? (v. 2)

What words describe Luke's preparation to write his own account? (v. 3)

To whom did he address his two-volume work of Luke and Acts? (v. 3)

Why did he record his two-volume account of events? (v. 4)

We will see Luke's investigative abilities, referenced in these verses, come into play throughout the Book of Acts as we discover the narratives, events, miracles, and speeches he recorded. Some of these he personally observed, but others required interviews with witnesses. Luke also highlighted the significance of the historical narrative both to the early church and to us today.

What have you investigated lately? Think of the last thing you researched on the Internet.

Recently I was considering which novels to take with me on a trip. I asked friends, checked to see if any of my favorite authors had something new, and also did some internet browsing. If we take time to research books, recipes, or DIY projects, imagine how seriously Luke took his task of writing an account of the birth of the church in his unique voice and style.

Luke's writings make up almost one-third of the New Testament. His Gospel is the longest New Testament book, with Acts coming in third in length. Luke's writing puts him on par with the apostle Paul for his breadth of vocabulary. However, their writings vary greatly when it comes to content.

Paul was a Jew, and while a few commentators disagree, most believe that Luke was a Gentile. His Greek name and use of the Septuagint (the Greek version of the Old Testament), as well as his vocabulary and style, reflect a Greek rather than Hebrew heritage. In addition, the fact that Paul greets Luke separately from the Jewish believers in Colossians 4:14 supports the idea that Luke was a Gentile.

Knowing that Luke likely was not a Jew gives us insight into his unique perspective of the gospel message and its spread from Jerusalem to the ends of the earth.

The New Testament includes four Gospel accounts by four different people: Matthew, Mark, Luke, and John. How do you think Luke's heritage as a Gentile provides a different point of view from the other three Gospels written by Jews?

Why do you think it is important to have a variety of perspectives when exploring any topic?

When I order commentaries, I include authors of different denominations and theological perspectives. I may not agree with all of their ideas, but I believe hearing varied voices brings balance. As we read through Acts in the coming weeks, we want to remember that a plurality of viewpoints can be good. We want to be stretched spiritually so that we may discover God in fresh ways.

Luke was an investigator, a Gentile, and an educated man who used his intellectual abilities to serve God. Though we know he was a doctor (Colossians 4:14), we find little mention of his personal narrative in the Scriptures. We will not get to know Luke through our study of Acts, but his account will give us a better understanding of his heroes, such as the apostles Peter and Paul. Luke's humility is evidenced through his emphasis on Christ, the Spirit, and the work of the apostles. He wrote to tell about others, not himself.

Read Luke 24:50-53 and Acts 1:1-3 and describe the continuity between Luke's two volumes. On whose story does Luke focus?

Luke wrote much about Jesus, yet he went further than any other Gospel writer in preparing an account of what happened after Jesus ascended. Warren Wiersbe wrote, "Imagine how confused you would be if, in reading your New Testament, you turned the last page of the gospel of John and discovered— Romans! 'How did the church get to Rome?' you would ask yourself; the answer is found in the book of Acts."[5] Luke was qualified to write this chronicle because he watched the church's missionary work firsthand.

Though he is rarely mentioned in the New Testament, we do find a few other clues about Luke in Paul's writings.

Read 2 Timothy 4:10-11 and Philemon 23-24 in the margin, and write below any additional information you glean about Luke:

Luke stayed with Paul when others left him. He was a faithful coworker in ministry. He didn't just write about spreading the gospel; he participated in it.

What new insights about the author of Acts have you learned today?

As we interact with the text of Acts each day in the coming weeks, I pray you will keep in mind that the author possessed investigative skills, a unique perspective as a Gentile, an educated yet humble approach, and faithful ministry experience. Acts is the living Word of God. May we approach it with an open mind and a willing heart.

Daily Wrap-Up

Each day we will look for God's initiatives and the early church's responses, reflecting on the same two questions:

- What is one way you noticed God at work in the chapter?
- How did the believers respond?

Some days God's work will be easily identifiable, such as when we read about healings, miracles, or other divine interventions. Other times, we will find

Demas has deserted me because he loves the things of this life and has gone to Thessalonica. Crescens has gone to Galatia, and Titus has gone to Dalmatia. Only Luke is with me. Bring Mark with you when you come, for he will be helpful to me in my ministry.
(2 Timothy 4:10-11)

Epaphras, my fellow prisoner in Christ Jesus, sends you his greetings. So do Mark, Aristarchus, Demas, and Luke, my co-workers.
(Philemon 23-24)

the Lord working behind the scenes. Because our study of Acts begins tomorrow, we will modify these questions for the author Luke today.

What is one way you noticed God at work in Luke's life as the author of Acts?

How did Luke respond to God's call?

God moved Luke to investigate and record the birth of the church after Jesus's ascension. Luke responded by doing diligent work so that we now have the opportunity to study Acts. Those who read Acts can fulfill Luke's intent, which is that people might be certain of the truth (Luke 1:4). Today we focused on this truth: *we can awaken to God's power because He has given us His Word.*

How would you summarize your personal takeaway from today's lesson?

Acts has the power to awaken us to truths we've known and new teachings we may have never heard before. Now, let's consider how we want God to awaken us through Luke's writings.

Take a moment to write a prayer below, asking the Lord to prepare your heart to receive all He has for you in this study.

Acts is a true story. A good story. I pray the Holy Spirit will use this story to intersect with your story and awaken you to see Him at work today!

Talk with God

Lord, I need Your Holy Spirit to guide me as I study Acts. Help me to learn what it means to sit at Your feet and listen. Help me to apply these ancient truths in my modern context. I can't do it without You. Amen.

Memory Verse Exercise

Read the Memory Verse on page 10 several times, and then fill in the blanks below as you recite it:

"But you will receive _____ when the Holy Spirit comes upon you. And you will be my _____, telling people about me everywhere—in _____, throughout Judea, in Samaria, and to the ends of the _____."

(Acts 1:8)

Day 2: Power in the Promise

Scripture Focus

Acts 1

After three hours on a school bus, we arrived at the waterpark for a youth retreat weekend. I'll admit I needed an attitude adjustment. Listening to the students in my group complain about not having their phones for two days was grating on my nerves. Once we got to our rooms, disagreement broke out about who had to sleep on the pull-out couches rather than the beds. My irritation level rose. I wanted to remind them how grateful they should be for a weekend away to stay in beautiful rooms, eat food prepared for them, hear amazing speakers, connect with a thousand other teenagers, and enjoy the waterpark. I knew my ranting wouldn't set a good tone, and I hustled the girls down to the first session.

Big Idea

We can awaken to God's power in waiting seasons because God keeps His promises.

As the worship began, I knew something needed to change in my heart. I confessed to the Lord my bad attitude. I complained about the ungrateful students. Then I asked Him to awaken in me a love for these girls. I prayed for them by name and asked Jesus to help me see them the way He does.

I can't explain what began to happen. Something inside me shifted. While I still had to deal with some difficult personalities, general immaturity, and more complaints about phones, I also was able to share my faith with these girls. On the last night, one of them asked if she could speak with me in private. With tears in her eyes, she asked if she could receive Christ personally in her life. I had the privilege of praying with her and sharing an eternal moment.

It was on that weekend retreat that I sensed from the Lord that the theme of this study should revolve around awakening to God in everyday life. He reminded me again that I can't serve Him in my human strength. His Spirit is necessary for spiritual life—mine and yours.

Can you remember a time in your life when God awakened you to see a person or situation through a new lens? If so, briefly share about it below:

Today as we open the pages of Acts, we will find the followers of Jesus in a significant pause as they wait for the gift that Jesus promised them. They were not to jump into activity without first waiting for God's promised Spirit.

Read Acts 1:1-11 and record what we learn about the Holy Spirit from Jesus:

These verses describe the period between Jesus's ascension into heaven and the coming of the Holy Spirit. We notice that:

- Jesus gave instructions to His disciples through the Holy Spirit,
- the Father would be the One sending the gift of the Spirit,
- Jesus said a baptism of the Holy Spirit was imminent, and
- power from the Holy Spirit would enable believers to be witnesses to the world.

I'm sure the disciples didn't know exactly what spiritual baptism and power would look like, but they gathered and waited for the promise to be fulfilled. I can imagine that after Jesus died, rose again, and then appeared to them over a forty-day period, they would have been antsy to start telling others about all that had happened. Yet Jesus told them to stay in Jerusalem and wait.

We can grow impatient and experience anxiety when God pushes the pause button in our lives. Sometimes we get ahead of Him by failing to wait for His leading.

What does waiting on the Holy Spirit look like in your life right now?

I often have thoughts and ideas that cause me to question whether they are my own or from the Spirit. When this happens, I pray, journal, sit quietly, and sometimes talk with godly friends before moving forward. I don't want to move without the Spirit's guidance, but I also don't want to lag behind because I'm distracted or apathetic. I know He wants to work in my life and yours. Here's some good news: *we can awaken to God's power in waiting seasons because God keeps His promises.*

In Acts 1, we see that while the disciples waited for the promise of the Spirit to be fulfilled, they asked questions, prepared, and prayed. These are three postures we can take when we experience significant pauses in our own lives.

Extra Insight: Baptism of the Holy Spirit

The concept of Holy Spirit baptism has caused much debate among followers of Jesus. Various groups believe differently about what it is and what it means. The word *baptized* in Acts 1:5 comes from the Greek word *baptizo*, which means "to dip repeatedly, to immerse, to submerge (of vessels sunk); to cleanse by dipping or submerging, to wash, to make clean with water, to wash one's self, bathe; to overwhelm."[7] While John the Baptist taught a baptism of repentance, Jesus commanded His disciples to go into all the world teaching and baptizing (Matthew 28:18-20). This practice usually involved immersing people in water as an outward expression of an inward change. When we consider what baptism of the Holy Spirit might look like, we can surmise that it hints toward a deep connection where we are fully submerged in His presence. What that looks like outwardly in our lives may vary.

---

1. Ask Questions

When we aren't sure what a passage of Scripture means or how we should handle a situation in our lives, we can ask questions.

Look back at Acts 1:6. What question were the disciples asking?

This was likely the question on everyone's mind. They had spent forty days with the resurrected Christ and knew that He had all authority and power. They wanted to see Him use it to right some wrongs! I can relate.

What wrongs would you love to see Jesus come and straighten out here on earth this week?

I can make a big list. We get pretty caught up with the matters of earth because we live here.

How did Jesus respond to their question in verse 7?

This is such a good reminder for me that God doesn't run everything by us. The Father sets the dates and times because He alone has that authority. He awakens us to trust Him with the divine calendar. Asking questions may not lead us to immediate answers, but it will help us align with God's bigger perspective. Questioning can lead us to deeper truths. God is not put off by our questions but invites us to ask and explore as we wrestle in our faith. The Lord loves us and remains in relationship with us through our questioning. He gives insight and also helps us learn to embrace mystery as some of our questions may never be answered.

2. Prepare

Jesus didn't directly answer the disciples' question but gave them a glimpse into what was coming so that they could prepare their minds and hearts.

Read verse 8 and fill in the blanks below:

They would receive _____.

So that they could be _____.

In Jerusalem, Judea, Samaria, and _____

_____.

This power was not given for worldly conquest or recompense for previous oppression. It would be provided so that they could be witnesses and tell others about Jesus—everywhere. Just as witnesses in court share with others what they saw and heard, witnesses for Jesus share with others what they've experienced personally with Jesus. Witnessing doesn't have to be a daunting practice where we shove Jesus down people's throats; it simply means telling others about Him.

Whether we are talking about Jesus with family, friends, coworkers, neighbors, or people we've just met, God says He will empower us through His Spirit. When I grow apathetic about the spiritual condition of those around me, it's like an indicator light on my spiritual dashboard telling me that I need a fresh awakening. It's not that I no longer care about people, but sometimes my own problems, enjoyment, and responsibilities can weaken my passion for those

Extra Insight

We are going to find the word *witness* used in some form over thirty-nine times in the Book of Acts, making it a prominent theme.[8]

who are lost and hurting. Knowing that the Lord will give us the power we need, we can prepare our hearts and minds to share our story of faith with others.

3. Pray

As I experienced that weekend on the youth retreat, one of the most effective ways for God to awaken me when I lack power or passion is through prayer. When I come to Him admitting my inabilities, that's when I see His strength in my weakness.

Read Acts 1:12-26, and write below what we find Jesus's followers doing in verse 14:

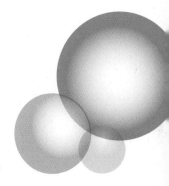

Extra Insight

"If one counts all possible references to the Spirit in Acts (fifty-nine), these constitute nearly a quarter of New Testament references to the Spirit; no other New Testament book has even half as many."[9]

We see that they were meeting together and constantly praying. I love that Luke mentions the women were part of this prayer meeting. One commentator notes, "The inclusion of women in the roster of the community would not have been missed by a second-century reader, as an indication that already we have a group which breaks barriers."[10] Prayer united them and prepared them as they waited for the promised Holy Spirit.

As believers, we already have the gift of the Holy Spirit, who lives inside us, but we must lean into His power and awaken to His promptings. Prayer reminds us that we need the power of the Holy Spirit and the help and encouragement of others to fulfill the God-sized tasks of sharing our faith and living holy lives in a difficult world.

Through prayer, we receive the Holy Spirit's power.
Through prayer, we are able to share with others about Jesus.
Through prayer, we unite with others.

What does your current prayer life look like? What helps you to connect with God?

What differences would you like to see in your connection and communication with God by the end of this study?

This is an area where I continually want to grow. I'm asking God to awaken me to deeper connection and communication with Him. I hope you are as well.

Consider the three responses of the disciples in Acts 1 and write any practical steps that you can take in these areas. (I have provided my own example for each.)

1. Ask Questions: What questions do you have right now?

Example: I'm asking God how I should focus my time in this season and what Holy Spirit baptism might look like in my life.

2. Prepare: How can you prepare for the work God is calling you to do?

Example: I'm taking foster care licensing classes in anticipation of what my husband and I sense God leading us to do.

3. Pray: What do you need to pray about right now?

Example: I'm praying that God would awaken me to Him in ways I can't even imagine.

A season of questioning, preparing, and praying preceded the action in the Book of Acts. As we awaken to the Lord in our everyday lives, we also encounter seasons of anticipation and preparation. If we want to see more spiritual action, we can implement these practices while we wait on God's perfect timing for movement in our lives.

Daily Wrap-Up

What is one way you noticed God at work in Acts 1?

How did the believers respond?

While it must have been deflating that Jesus was no longer with His disciples in physical form, He ascended to heaven with a promise to send the third person of the Trinity, the Holy Spirit. God's people responded to His instructions by asking questions, preparing, and praying. We learn from them to awaken to God's power even during waiting seasons.

Today we focused on this truth: *we can awaken to God's power in waiting seasons because God keeps His promises.*

How would you summarize your personal takeaway from today's lesson?

I'm so glad the Lord awakened me to His love for the students on that youth group trip. As a result of that experience, I want to learn to lean into God's power instead of attempting to conjure up my own. Even in waiting seasons, we can ask questions, prepare, and pray knowing that God will supply the power to accomplish His purposes in every situation.

Talk with God

Lord, help me to learn from the early Christians to wait well. I don't want to get ahead of Your Spirit's work, but I also don't want to lag behind. Show me where I can ask questions, prepare, and be more devoted in prayer when You hit the pause button in my life. Amen.

Memory Verse Exercise

Read the Memory Verse on page 10 several times, and then fill in the blanks below as you recite it:

"But _____ will receive _____ when the _____ _____ comes upon you. And _____ will be my _____, telling people about me everywhere—in _____, throughout _____, in Samaria, and to the ends of the _____."

(Acts 1:8)

Day 3: Power in the Holy Spirit

In the late 1990s, our culture became fascinated with watching television shows featuring real people experiencing real life. From scenarios involving deserted islands to dating life, reality television doesn't fully live up to its name because we never really know how much of the relationships and experiences

Scripture Focus

Acts 2

Big Idea

We can awaken to God because He sent His Spirit to empower us.

we are witnessing are staged. Although no one is likely filming us on a regular basis, we too can live an edited version of the Christian life. What I mean is that sometimes we live like what is real isn't actually real. For example,

- We know Jesus paid for our sin on the cross, but sometimes we live in shame.
- We know God has given us power through the Holy Spirit, but often we live defeated lives.
- We know God is with us, but we feel completely alone.

Have you felt a disconnect from the promises of God and your daily life recently or in the past? If so, describe your experience below:

I'm constantly seeking to reconcile my theology and my reality. I want to live the truths about God that I know from Scripture, but I struggle. I don't believe I'm the only one. We Christians don't seem to be enjoying peace and unity these days. When I scroll through social media, I wonder what the world thinks of us as a result of our online presence. I'm asking God to awaken me to experience the power I already have through His Spirit, and I hope you are as well. Today we will focus on this truth: *we can awaken to God because He sent His Spirit to empower us.*

God's power can transform our lives and unify us as believers. In Genesis 11, we read about the Tower of Babel where the Lord confused the people's language and dispersed them over the earth. After that event, we find references in the Old Testament to a coming day when God's people would again be united through His Spirit (Ezekiel 36:26-32). God progressively revealed His plan in shadows and hints that came together on the day of Pentecost when, as many scholars suggest, languages unified rather than separated people.[11]

Read Acts 2:1-13 and summarize what happened in your own words below (write a few sentences or use bullet points):

By the first century, Pentecost had become a time to commemorate the giving of the commandments on Mount Sinai.[12] How fitting that the Lord chose to pour out His Spirit on the day when Judaism celebrated the giving of the law. Many scholars believe this fulfilled His promise to bring God's people back together after the years of confusion and dispersion. When the Holy Spirit controls the lives of believers, we see His fruit growing in "love, joy, peace, patience, kindness, goodness, faithfulness, gentleness, and self-control" (Galatians 5:22-23).

How have you experienced God's supernatural fruit found in Galatians 5:22-23 in your relationships?

Just this week, the Spirit gave me self-control to hold my tongue in a conversation. The Holy Spirit awakens responses in us that run contrary to our selfish natures. When this happens, He is unleashed to heal the fractures in our families, friendships, local church bodies, and online conversations. Sometimes He uses subtle nudges, but in Acts 2 we see obvious displays of power.

What are some audible and visible evidences of the Holy Spirit in Acts 2:2-4?

In these verses, we discover three signs of God's presence found in the Old Testament now combined in the Holy Spirit's coming. Wind (Ezekiel 37:9-14), fire (Exodus 3:2-5), and inspired speech (Numbers 11:26-29) confirmed the validity of the Spirit's miraculous work.[13] Just as Jesus performed miracles to get people's attention and authenticate His ministry, so the coming of the Holy Spirit was marked by supernatural events that the Israelites would have associated with their spiritual history. You would think that after such an incredible display, surely everyone would believe that God was at work.

What two reactions of the witnesses are recorded in Acts 2:12-13?

1.

2.

While I've often wished for God to awaken us to His presence through visible displays such as this one at Pentecost, I know that even if He did, some would not listen. Throughout the Book of Acts, we will find that the Lord chooses to use His people to share His message. Through the power of the Holy Spirit living inside us, we can share the news about Christ's death and resurrection with a hurting world. The fruit of God's Spirit pouring forth from our lives provides a witness of God's love and grace to those around us. Often it is our lives as much as or more than our words that attracts others to God.

What initially drew you to desire a relationship with God?

I'm guessing that it likely didn't involve seeing wind, fire, or people speaking in other languages but had something to do with another person. Maybe a parent, friend, or preacher shared a message that awakened your connection with your Creator. In the next half of chapter 2, we will find the apostle Peter boldly explaining from the Old Testament Scriptures the promises God made regarding the Holy Spirit. In yesterday's lesson the disciples asked questions, prepared for action, and prayed. Now, the time has come for action.

Read Acts 2:14–41 and number the events below from 1–5 as they occur in the passage:

_____ A. About three thousand believed what Peter said and were baptized.

_____ B. Peter quoted King David and told the crowd that Jesus is now seated at God's right hand in the highest heaven.

_____ C. Peter's words pierced their hearts, and they asked, "What should we do?"

_____ D. Peter shouted to the crowd that no one was drunk, but that the words of the prophet Joel were being fulfilled with the pouring out of God's Spirit.

_____ E. Peter told each person that they should repent of their sins, turn to God, and be baptized and then they would receive the Holy Spirit.

The apostle Peter used the writings of the prophet Joel and King David to explain the fulfillment of God's promise of the Holy Spirit. The message pierced the hearts of the people, and they asked this question in response, "Brothers, what should we do?" (Acts 2:37). This question resonates with me. I wonder if it does with you as well.

We no longer live in confusion and isolation. God has filled us with His Spirit if we have believed and received His gospel personally. Yet the "confusion" we read about at the Tower of Babel still seems to permeate the church. We fight on social media, form factions against our leaders, and lack the unity we should enjoy through God's Spirit. Sisters, what should we do?

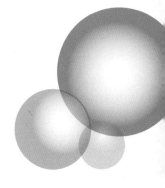

Peter was intentional to say in his reply to the crowd in Acts 2 that his answer was not only for the original audience but also for those "far away" or those yet to be born. That's us! Like them, we must turn from our sins to God and receive the Holy Spirit (Acts 2:38). This word *receive* is the verb *lambano* in Greek, which means "to take; to take with the hand, lay hold of, any person or thing in order to use it; to take up a thing to be carried; to take upon one's self."[14]

While God freely gave the gifts of His Son and His Spirit, we must actively receive them. You may wonder what this looks like. Let's see how some of the people responded to the Spirit's leading.

Read Acts 2:42-47 and circle any of the words below that describe their behavior:

teaching	being apathetic	enjoying fellowship
praying	watching TV	practicing generosity
praising God	shopping online	sharing meals
being anxious	experiencing awe	criticizing others
worshipping at the Temple	meeting together in homes	arguing over minor issues
enjoying goodwill	sharing with those in need	performing signs and wonders

These are some of the ways receiving God's Spirit evidenced itself in the believers' lives. Perhaps awakening to the power of God's Spirit might increase these practices in our lives as well, so that our spiritual communities will more closely align to the infant church we read about in Acts 2. That would be the best reality show for the watching world! The problem of disunity among us still lingers, but the antidote remains the same—receiving God's Spirit and allowing Him to change the reality of our lives.

Daily Wrap-Up

What is one way you noticed God at work in Acts 2?

How did the believers respond?

God sent the Holy Spirit with wind, fire, and inspired speech. His disciples preached from Scripture, and many responded to the miracles with belief and baptism. They devoted themselves to teaching, fellowship, and prayer.

Today we focused on this truth: *we can awaken to God because He sent His Spirit to empower us.*

How would you summarize your personal takeaway from today's lesson?

I was convicted and challenged at how much the early church gathered, shared, and prayed together. This week I'm going to invite another family over and focus that time on uplifting conversation rather than complaining about all that is happening in the world. Perhaps you had a very different takeaway. I love that the Holy Spirit works with each of us in unique ways. One thing we all can do as followers of Jesus is to pray for unity among believers through God's Holy Spirit, asking Him to awaken us to His presence in our midst.

Talk with God

Lord, Your church is a hot mess sometimes. We fight and slander one another. Help us to live in the reality of Your Holy Spirit and rediscover the unity of the early church. I invite You, Holy Spirit—fully and passionately—to let transformation start with me today. Amen.

Memory Verse Exercise

Read the Memory Verse on page 10 several times, and then fill in the blanks below as you recite it:

"But _____ will _____ _____ when the _____ _____ comes upon you. And _____ _____ be my _____, telling _____ about me everywhere—in _____, throughout _____, in _____, and to the ends of the _____."

(Acts 1:8)

Day 4: Power in the Name of Jesus

Scripture Focus

Acts 3

Several years ago, I visited Nashville with a group of girlfriends. One of the gals in our group texted a friend who owned several restaurants downtown to ask for a recommendation. Her friend directed us to a place and said to mention her name at the door. To our surprise, when we gave her name we were ushered into a special section with VIP treatment. Servers brought out complimentary platters of food and told of us about the famous musicians who had occupied our seats the night before. I sat in awe of the unexpected blessings we received just by dropping a name.

Big Idea

We can awaken to God because there is power in the name of Jesus.

Extra Insight

"The stated times for prayer in Judaism were (1) early in the morning, in connection with the morning sacrifice; (2) at the ninth hour of the day, in connection with the evening sacrifice; and (3) at sunset."[15]

Have you ever known someone whose name afforded you special privileges? If so, describe the situation below:

Today as we study Acts 3, we are going to discover the power of name-dropping for every Christ-follower. After Jesus ascended into heaven and sent the Holy Spirit to empower the early church, the believers still experienced the power of His name. We don't have to live powerless lives because there is power in the name of Jesus.

Read Acts 3:1-11 and fill in the details of the story below:

Which two disciples were involved? (v. 1)

_____ and _____

Where were they going? (v. 1) _____

Whom did they encounter at the gate? (v. 2) _____

What was he asking for? (v. 3) _____

What did Peter give him instead? (v. 6) _____

By whose name did Peter accomplish this? (v. 6)

_____

What actions was the lame man now able to perform? (v. 8)

_____, _____, _____

What stands out to you about this story?

Here are some thoughts I had as I studied:

- **God can use anyone to do anything He chooses.** Peter and John had been partners in a fishing business (Luke 5:10), but it seems that Peter may have compared himself to and possibly competed with John at times (John 21:21). Now, they were working together to build the church. Anything is possible in our lives and relationships too!
- **God calls us to run to the messes rather than avoid them.** Sin has put every one of us into the "messes" category. Peter got the beggar's attention because he made eye contact. I'm guessing many people avoided this lame man's gaze. As we saw in Acts 2, Peter had just preached and seen three thousand people turn to God, yet he wasn't above sharing the good news one person at a time. It encourages me to consider the ways I can seek rather than avoid those around me who have needs.
- **Church stuff shouldn't consume all our energy.** This incident follows the church's sharing their resources that was explained at the end of Acts 2. I don't want to become so focused on my fellow Christians that I forget about those suffering with physical and spiritual needs outside the church.
- **Jesus's name has power.** The healed beggar is proof that Jesus really is alive. Isaiah 35:6 foretold that "the lame will leap like a deer." The man clung to the disciples, but they were just the agents bearing the name of the One with authority. The name wasn't magical (the disciples distanced themselves from any kind of sorcery as we will see in Acts 8; 13; and 19), but Jesus continued to act powerfully through those who called upon His name.

Of these four principles from the passage, which one resonates most personally with you right now? Why?

Extra Insight

Solomon's colonnade or portico was an outdoor hallway on the eastern side of the Temple that became a common place for believers in Jesus to gather (Acts 5:12).[16]

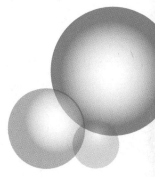

I'm asking myself how the power of Jesus's name can be more of a reality in my life. I want to awaken to this truth so that I begin to regularly apply this power to my prayers for others and my struggles with sin. If Peter could heal a lame man through Jesus's name, I know that my apathy, distraction, and weariness are not too big for the power of His name!

"In Semitic thought, a name does not just identify or distinguish a person; it expresses the very nature of his being."[18]

Read Acts 3:12-26 and write in your own words the call to action Peter made in verse 19 to the crowd that gathered:

Peter saw the opportunity to preach after Jesus's power healed the lame man. Remember that He was in the Temple, so the crowd would have consisted of Jews or proselytes who had converted to Judaism.

What Old Testament figures did Peter mention to convince the crowd that Jesus was the Messiah? (vv. 13, 22, 24)

Peter knew his audience. He went all the way back to Abraham, Isaac, and Jacob, aligning Jesus with the God of the patriarchs the audience venerated. Then He spoke of Moses and Samuel, weaving together the story of promise and fulfillment in Jesus so they might understand His identity as servant and prophet. Many had been expecting the Messiah to come as conqueror, but instead Jesus was the suffering servant the prophet Isaiah had spoken about (Isaiah 52:13-15).

It was Jesus's name that healed a man they knew to be crippled from birth—the same Jesus the Jews brought to the Romans to be crucified. This would seem to be discouraging news for Peter's hearers since it meant they not only had failed to recognize the Messiah but also had murdered Him. But Peter's message didn't end in shame. He proclaimed that it wasn't too late because they had not out-sinned the grace of God even by killing His own Son!

Jesus said, "Father, forgive them, for they don't know what they are doing."
(Luke 23:34)

Read Luke 23:34 in the margin and summarize Jesus's attitude toward His torturers.

While Jesus might have directed this prayer toward the Roman soldiers, His grace extended to those who had pressured the Romans to act. The power that we find in Jesus's name brings grace instead of retribution and healing instead of brokenness. Peter spoke of blessing and times of refreshing that would come from the Lord for those who would turn from their sin and turn to God.

Those who heard Peter's message were not beyond saving, and neither are we. We can look around at our world and our daily struggles and feel powerless. In Acts 3, we find a God who never gives up on us no matter our past offenses. The disciples had awakened to the power of Jesus's name, and so can we.

I sometimes wonder why we don't see as many miracles and healings today as we find in the days of the early church. Some say that God used these signs to establish the church and authenticate the message. Others propose that we receive little because we believe little. What we do know is that God is still working and healing. We can ask in His name as we pray.

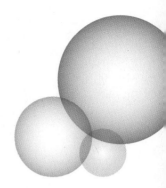

Read the following words of Jesus spoken during His earthly ministry and draw a circle around the words *my name* wherever you see them together:

You can ask for anything in my name, and I will do it, so that the Son can bring glory to the Father. Yes, ask me for anything in my name, and I will do it!

(John 14:13-14)

You didn't choose me. I chose you. I appointed you to go and produce lasting fruit, so that the Father will give you whatever you ask for, using my name.

(John 15:16)

At that time you won't need to ask me for anything. I tell you the truth, you will ask the Father directly, and he will grant your request because you use my name. You haven't done this before. Ask, using my name, and you will receive, and you will have abundant joy.

(John 16:23-24)

How would you summarize the point Jesus is trying to convey?

Jesus told us to ask God for what we need using His name. Where do you need power today? Perhaps you are battling unforgiveness, jealous thoughts, a food addiction, or an apathetic attitude. Wherever you are feeling weak, Jesus invites us to ask God for power using His name!

Write below a personal request using the name of Jesus:

Today I'm asking God for greater faith and understanding. I don't want to continue to study Acts unaffected by the power of Jesus's name for my battles with small things, such as junk food and my thought life, as well as big things, such as fear and disobedience. His name can heal and turn us back from sin!

Daily Wrap-Up

What is one way you noticed God at work in Acts 3?

How did the believers respond?

The power of Jesus's name healed a man lame from birth. Peter used this opportunity to preach the power of Jesus's name for those who would turn from their sin to God. The crippled man responded by praising God. We may or may not have been physically healed, but every follower of Christ has experienced spiritual healing from the disease of sin. We can praise God because we find power in His name.

Today we focused on this truth: *we can awaken to God because there is power in the name of Jesus.*

How would you summarize your personal takeaway from today's lesson?

We can awaken to God's power as we begin to make requests in Jesus's name. It's not a magic word, but His name carries His authority and power. My friends and I were lavished with privileges when we used the restaurant owner's name. Jesus's name carries more weight than any other authoritative name we might know. He isn't merely a past historical figure but our living hope. Speaking His name acknowledges that He can transform our lives and heal our brokenness.

Talk with God

Lord, I want to see You work as You did in the early church. Cultures change, but Your message does not. May I never grow numb to the power of Your name. Jesus, Your name is above every other name. Help me to understand Your power so that I might bring glory and honor to You! Amen.

Memory Verse Exercise

Read the Memory Verse on page 10 several times, and then fill in the blanks below as you recite it:

"But _____ will _____ _____ when the _____

_____ comes _____ you. _____ _____ _____

be _____ _____, telling _____ about me

_____—in _____, throughout

_____, in _____, and _____ the _____ of the

_____."

(*Acts* 1:8)

Day 5: Power in Prayer

All week we've been talking about awakening to God's power. We've learned about the power found in His Word, His promises, His Spirit, and His name, yet so often in our daily experiences, we feel more powerless than powerful. Sometimes I lack discipline and get distracted and then feel shame for my perceived "spiritual defeat." Maybe you can relate with my need to awaken to God's power.

In which areas of your life do you have a greater awareness of your need to experience God's power?

Many times, I lack passion because of what I'm *not* doing rather than what I *am* doing. When my prayer life is dry, rote, or inconsistent, it can be an indicator that I need to awaken to God. Lack of time isn't usually the issue. Prayerlessness seeps into my life as I slowly begin to rely on my own abilities rather than recognize my dependence on God. Awakening to my own limitations and needs often leads me to awaken to God through prayer.

We've seen this week that the early church experienced God's power.

As you reflect on our study of Acts 1–3 this week, what powerful acts of God and responses of God's people have stood out to you?

Scripture Focus

Acts 4

Big Idea

We can awaken to God's power because we have direct access to Him through prayer.

Jesus ascended into heaven. The Holy Spirit descended with wind, fire, and inspired languages. A lame man began to walk. We witnessed the disciples speaking, praying, sharing, and experiencing unity as many who heard the message about Jesus believed. Today we will find that not everyone was thrilled about these powerful encounters. We'll also learn about a practice the church utilized when they faced opposition.

Read Acts 4:1-22 and answer the following questions:

Who confronted Peter and John? (v. 1)

Extra Insight

"It is interesting that, although the Pharisees were the group most opposed to Jesus during his ministry, in Acts they are almost friendly to the church, while the Sadducees (who do not figure in the Gospels until the last days of Jesus) have become the leaders of the opposition."[19]

Why were they disturbed? (v. 2)

How many men (not including women and children) now believed in Jesus? (v. 4)

What question did the council have for Peter and John? (v. 7)

How did Peter answer it? (v. 10)

How did the council describe Peter and John? (v. 13)

What did the council decide to do with them? (v. 18)

What did Peter and John say in response? (v. 20)

The council saw Peter and John as ordinary men except for the fact that they had been with Jesus. Their power was not their own. Being with Jesus on earth and then being filled with the Holy Spirit empowered them to do things they could not have accomplished of their own accord. This is the secret of powerful Christian living. Ordinary people can be used in extraordinary ways when God's power flows through them.

Peter and John believed Jesus's message. In doing this, they set aside their human reasoning and exchanged it for faith in God's way. Witnessing miracles and hearing Jesus teach strengthened their faith so that they could believe. By spending time with Him, they were forever changed in their thinking and values.

How do disciples today learn about Jesus?

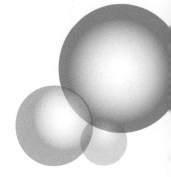

We don't have Jesus with us in physical form. Although it was clear that these men had been with Jesus, we also notice that Peter's speech came as a result of being filled with the Holy Spirit (Acts 4:8). Jesus actually had told His disciples that it would be better for Him to go so that He could send the Holy Spirit (John 16:7).

What enables ordinary people today to be used by God in extraordinary ways?

Through God's Spirit, we can allow God to use us to serve, love, and share His message with others. Apart from His power, we can get caught in a cycle of trying and failing. I want to be more in tune with God's Spirit who dwells within me, but sometimes I'm reluctant or unsure. I wonder if you have ever felt that way. I wish I could talk with Peter about how he experienced connection with God's Spirit. What I do know is that prayer played an important role.

Read Acts 4:23-37 and answer the following questions:

What was the believers' first response to the opposition? (v. 24)

What happened after the prayer? (v. 31)

How did the prayer impact their relationships? (v. 32)

What stands out to you regarding the elements of the prayer found in verses 24-30?

I noticed that they prayed...

- **Together.** Verse 24 says they "lifted their voices together in prayer." Commentators suggest they likely didn't say these exact words at the same time but, rather, Luke summarized the content of their prayer.
- **With reverence.** They addressed God as the Sovereign Lord, the Creator of heaven and earth. Powerful prayers in Scripture often start by praising God and recognizing His position of authority.
- **Using Scripture.** The believers prayed using the words of Psalm 2:1-2 in this passage. In addition, commentators note that the structure for the prayer seems to be modeled after the prayer of Hezekiah in Isaiah 37:16-20.[20] They not only prayed Scripture but also drew from biblical prayers for their format and tone. We can look to the Bible for content, examples, and inspiration for our own conversations with God.
- **For spiritual favor.** They asked for boldness rather than divine protection. Often my prayer list is filled to the brim with requests for quick fixes, but the early Christians prayed for spiritual rather than circumstantial favor. Phillips Brooks wrote, "Do not pray for easy lives. Pray to be stronger men and women. Do not pray for tasks equal to your powers. Pray for powers equal to your tasks."[21]

When I read passages like this, I wonder why I don't talk to God more. Prayer has power. It connects us to God and to fellow believers. It realigns us to what really matters. It awakens us to supernatural possibilities.

Sometimes, though, prayer can seem like a cop-out. When someone is going through something difficult and we say we will pray for them, it may not feel like enough. We wish we could really *do* something to assuage their pain. But here is the thing: prayer *is* doing something—a big something. Warren Wiersbe said this, "Prayer is not an escape from responsibility; it is our *response* to God's *ability*. True prayer energizes us for service and battle."[22] Prayer often becomes the catalyst that propels us into action as we are led by the Holy Spirit. Prayer connects us with the heart of God, which changes us and empowers us to be God's hands and feet in the world.

What are some things that inhibit your prayer life?

For me, the greatest inhibitor to prayer is a lack of faith. When I truly believe that prayer has transformational power—first within me and my life and then within the lives of others—I pray. But when I drift into self-sufficiency and buy into the lies that God won't meet me in prayer in a lifegiving way and that my prayers won't make much difference in my life or the lives of others, I either stop praying or go through the motions with little fervor. One way to reignite our passion for talking with the Lord is to pray about our struggle to pray. I know it sounds crazy. But we can talk to God about our lack of longing to connect with and talk to Him.

God knows all about our daily routines, the games we play on our phones, the shows we watch, our music, and also the concerns we are trying to work out in our heads. He understands our struggle with focus and self-discipline. We can ask Him to awaken our desire for divine connection and conversation.

Today's lesson purposely contains fewer words on the page so that you have time to write more words of your own . . . in prayer.

Take some time now to talk with God by using the prompts below, or write your own prayer as you desire (feel free to use a separate piece of paper or journal if you need more room):

God, You are great. I praise You because You are:

God, You know how I struggle with sin. I confess my need for You in these areas:

Lord, You have done great things. I thank You for:

Jesus, here are the concerns I am bringing before You now:

Holy Spirit, I want to surrender more of my heart and life to You so I can deepen my experience of Your love and allow You to use me powerfully to share that love with others. I will wait quietly now for awareness of your presence, guidance, and direction. Fill me with Your Spirit and speak to me. (Spend five minutes being still in God's presence. Write any impressions from your quiet time below.):

In Jesus's name. Amen.

Daily Wrap-Up

What is one way you noticed God at work in Acts 4?

How did the believers respond?

Today we found God at work in a variety of ways. He sovereignly allowed Peter and John to be questioned and then released by the Jewish council (v. 21). He also shook the meeting place after the believers prayed. Peter and John obeyed God rather than human authorities, and the entire church responded with unified prayer (v. 24). Acts 4 reminds us that prayer is a powerful practice that connects us to a powerful God!

Today we focused on this truth: *we can awaken to God's power because we have direct access to Him through prayer.*

How would you summarize your personal takeaway from today's lesson?

In just our first week in Acts, we've discovered that God doesn't want us to live powerless lives but to fully experience His power. Jesus died on the cross and rose again in victory. His Spirit moved Luke to record His Word to encourage us. He has given us His Holy Spirit to empower us, and His promises sustain us in waiting seasons. Jesus now sits at the right hand of the Father in heaven, and His name carries the weight of His authority and has power in our lives. Through prayer, we can wake up from our spiritual sleepiness and connect with our powerful God.

Talk with God

Lord, I struggle to consistently seek You in prayer. Forgive me for thinking I can live a spiritual life apart from You. Awaken in me the desire to pray. I know that You alone have the power to bring hope in my life and our world. Make me more aware of my dependence on You through prayer so that I might experience Your presence and power in my everyday life. Amen.

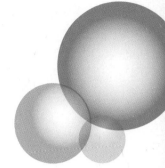

Memory Verse Exercise

Read the Memory Verse on page 10 several times, and then fill in the blanks below as you recite it:

"_____ _____ will _____ _____ _____ the _____ _____ _____ _____ you. _____ _____ ____ be __ _____, _____ _____ about me _____—in _____, _____ _____, in _____, _____ __ the _____ of the _____."

(Acts 1:8)

Weekly Wrap-Up

Review the Big Idea for each day, and then write any personal application that comes to mind.

Day 1: Power of the Pen

Big Idea: we can awaken to God's power because He has given us His
Word.

Personal Application:_____

_____

Day 2: Power in the Promise

Big Idea: we can awaken to God's power in waiting seasons because
God keeps His promises.

Personal Application:_____

_____

Day 3: Power in the Holy Spirit

Big Idea: we can awaken to God because He sent His Spirit to
empower us.

Personal Application:_____

_____

Day 4: Power in the Name of Jesus

Big Idea: we can awaken to God because there is power in the name
of Jesus.

Personal Application:_____

_____

Day 5: Power in Prayer

Big Idea: we can awaken to God's power because we have direct
access to Him through prayer.

Personal Application:_____

_____

Video Viewer Guide: Week 1

We can't manufacture _____ _____ _____, but we can awaken to _____ _____ through His Spirit!

We read Acts not for _____— but for _____!

The Holy Spirit fills us with the _____ _____ ____ _____.

Acts 1:8   Acts 4:31

Acts 2:17-18   Acts 2:42

Acts 2:38-39   Acts 2:44-47

Acts 1:14

To awaken to the Spirit, we must awaken to _____.

Faith is not a _____.

To awaken to the Spirit, we must awaken to _____.

Week 2

Awakening to God's Message

Acts 5–9

Memory Verse

And every day, in the Temple and from house to house, they continued to teach and preach this message: "Jesus is the Messiah."

(Acts 5:42)

Day 1: The Message of Life

After a night of intermittent sleep, I woke up feeling groggy and unsettled. I went through my morning routine, including some vague prayers and unfocused Bible reading where my mind wandered. I answered a few emails, organized some paperwork, and participated in an online meeting, Then I wandered into the kitchen to make lunch, but my eyes were drawn to the large screen above the mantle. I began to make internal justifications why I deserved an afternoon off from work, distracting myself with a television show.

- I had work to do, but I could find another time to squeeze it in without missing deadlines.
- I didn't sleep well, so I wouldn't be efficient if I tried to work.
- I had had minor surgery the previous week and probably needed some additional rest (even though I had been back to normal for days).

Don't hear me say there is never a time to take an afternoon off, but this wasn't a case of needing self-care. You see, I struggle with watching too much television. Maybe it's not your brand of escape; perhaps you like to distract yourself with social media, novels, online games, or something else. All of these things can be helpful tools, but they also can be coping mechanisms that get out of balance in our lives. If we aren't careful, they can become our masters rather than our servants. We must pay attention when isolated incidents of self-distraction become patterns of behavior.

Can you identify any activity in your life that threatens to become your master if you don't stay on guard? (If you are having trouble answering this, think of your self-talk regarding limits you set for yourself but struggle to maintain.)

This week our focus will be awakening to God's message. We have access to online resources, libraries of books, and Bibles as never before. The problem isn't always ignorance of God's message but the abundance of other messages that threaten to crowd it out. Seemingly innocent messages can distract us and allow subtle lies to seep into our thinking. Discernment can help us to recognize counterfeit messages that are woven into the fabric of our culture and appeal to our sinful nature. We can learn from the early church to separate truth from deception.

Scripture Focus

Acts 5

Big Idea

We want to awaken to God's message because it's the only one that really matters.

Extra Insight

In Acts 5, we find the first appearance of the word *church*, which is the Greek word *ekklēsia*.[1]

As we open the text today, we will see that the early Christians weren't just singing "Kumbaya" and sharing all their possessions.

Read Acts 5:1-11 and record an insight that strikes you and a question this situation raises for you:

Insight:

Question:

Each of us may have been struck by different aspects of this story, but my question is this: *Why such a harsh punishment? Where is the grace?*

Luke was careful not to idealize the early Christians, portraying them as perfect people. They were human. Ananias and his wife conspired to lie to the church. We learn from them that we can try to deceive people, but we can't deceive the Holy Spirit.

Glance back at Acts 4:36-37 and guess why Ananias and Sapphira might have conspired to lie.

It's possible they wanted the accolades that came with generosity without the sacrifice that accompanies it. While it may be hard to accept the severity of the lesson, we find that God used their example to warn the early church about the dangers of half-truths.

How would you summarize God's message through this incident that Luke chose to include in Acts?

You might have phrased it any number of ways, but the principle we find here is this: *God takes deception seriously*. Even subtle lies can affect and infect a spiritual community.

How did the people respond to this message according to Acts 5:11?

How does this message apply today? What are some common subtle lies of our culture (consider the messages we receive through our mailboxes, screens, and even conversations)?

Here are a few I notice on a regular basis:

- "It's normal to have sex before marriage." (Many sitcoms today normalize this behavior.)
- "The most important thing in life is to love yourself." (Check out the best-selling books and products.)
- "You deserve comfort and security." (Seen any ads lately?)

To awaken His church, God illustrated the severity of deception in a very tangible way. While we may wrestle with the method, let's not miss the message! Deception leads to death—not in the physical sense like Ananias and Sapphira experienced, but in other profound ways. Lies kill relationships, dreams, and hope. But the good news of God's message leads to life. Abundant life. That's why He longs for us to live in the truth and not be suckered into the culture's consuming counterfeits.

Let's get to that life-giving message now.

Read Acts 5:12-42 and answer the following questions, summarizing the answers in your own words:

What motivated the Sadducees to oppose the apostles? (v. 17)

What simple message did Peter and the apostles share with them? (vv. 29-32)

What advice did Gamaliel offer regarding that message? (vv. 38-39)

How did the apostles approach God's message regarding Jesus? (vv. 41-42)

Extra Insight

The apostle Paul studied under the Jewish law teacher Gamaliel (Acts 22:3).

The simple message that Jesus died on a cross and rose from the dead so that Israel (and all people) would believe in Him as Savior, repent of their sin, and receive forgiveness caused a big stir. The disciples' power of healing in Jesus's name threatened the popularity and position of the Jewish spiritual leaders. Rather than investigate the message as Luke did, they fretted over their reputations as Ananias likely did.

Ananias and Sapphira wanted others to think highly of them. The Sadducees wanted the crowd's favor. Yet Gamaliel's words remind us that God's message of life cannot be stopped. That brings me hope in a world where truth often seems distorted and diluted.

Can you see the theme Luke wove together in what seems like two unrelated incidents? God's message leads to life. Deception leads to death. Let's bring these truths a little closer to home.

Think through your typical day, and make a check mark beside those things that you come into contact with regularly:

__ Radio	__ Magazines	__ Podcasts
__ Television	__ Online videos	__ Audiobooks
__ Movies	__ Phone	__ Books
__ Social media	__ Tablet	__ Online games

These tools can be servants or masters in our lives. These mediums can bring messages of life but also messages of deception so we need discernment in our handling of them. We also want to limit our use of these tools so we have more margin and quiet to hear God's messages through His Word and His Spirit. Think about your patterns. Consider whether any of the messages you consume on a regular basis are embedded with worldly half-truths or untruths that might be affecting you.

Write below any adjustments that you sense would be beneficial in awakening to God's message in your life:

After my television-filled day, I knew some changes were in order. I didn't want to be legalistic and try to manage my temptations. Yet I found that as I spent time in honest prayer, the Holy Spirit nudged me to set some personal guardrails. Like braces that realign the teeth for a certain amount of time, I set some boundaries regarding my media consumption. This meant setting limits

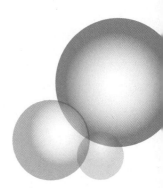

on when I would use media and for how long. I also deleted some social media apps from my phone, forcing me to view them only on my laptop. Some television shows aren't good for my soul as they continually espouse messages that don't align with God's Word. I chose to stop watching them and found some better alternatives. Awakening to God's messages with some small changes in my daily routine has brought clarity and joy. These changes created more space for me to listen to God and focus on more uplifting messages.

I'm praying that God's Spirit awakens *you* to His messages in your everyday life.

Daily Wrap-Up

What is one way you noticed God at work in Acts 5?

How did the believers respond?

It blows me away that Ananias and Sapphira died so suddenly, and that God released the apostles from prison in a supernatural way. His people responded by showing awe and gratefulness and by going from house to house teaching and preaching the message about Jesus!

Today we focused on this truth: *we want to awaken to God's message because it's the only one that really matters*.

How would you summarize your personal takeaway from today's lesson?

When God's message of life through Christ takes first place in our lives, we realize that it is the only message that matters! Our response to this message leads us either to life or death. Whether you've had a string of days like the one I shared earlier where you're struggling to limit or filter the messages you're consuming or you are enjoying victory in this area, we can all grow by awakening more and more to God's message of life.

Talk with God

Lord, I sometimes struggle to filter the many messages of our culture. Help me identify and turn away from lies. Purify my heart so that I want your fame rather than the approval of others. I am human, Lord. Awaken me to Your message of life throughout this day! Amen.

Memory Verse Exercise

Read the Memory Verse on page 44 several times, and then fill in the blanks below as you recite it:

And every day, in the _____ and from house to _____, they continued to teach and preach this message: "Jesus is the _____."

(Acts 5:42)

Day 2: The Priority of the Message

Scripture Focus

Acts 6

Big Idea

Internal and external forces threaten God's message, so we must prioritize the teaching of God's Word.

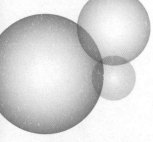

Extra Insight

"Problems give us the opportunity to examine our ministries and discover what changes must be made."[2]

My mind raced on the drive home from a church event. I had enjoyed meeting and talking with new women, and even praying with several of them. The reason for my inner turmoil revolved around a woman I had met whose views on the core message of the gospel were different from my own. We didn't argue at all. Instead, I asked a lot of questions and listened. Though I think she and others I know who embrace similar views are incredible people, the alarm bells of truth rang loudly inside as I processed our conversation afterward.

Jesus was a perfect balance of truth and grace. As we look at historical movements of the church, we see that the pendulum has swung back and forth from an overemphasis on truth to an overemphasis on grace. Today's reading will reveal the importance of both grace and truth.

Read Acts 6:1-7 and draw a line to connect each statement to the correct ending:

As the church grew rapidly, they experienced	A. Hebrew speaking believers.
The Greek-speaking believers (Hellenists) accused the	B. oversee a food program.
The main issue was	C. the church grew in number.
So, the twelve apostles called a	D. unequal aid to widows.
They decided the apostles needed to focus on	E. meeting.
They selected seven godly men to	F. prayer and teaching.
God's messages continued to spread and	G. rumblings of discontent.

Answers: 1.G, 2.A, 3.D, 4.E, 5.F, 6.B, 7.C

What insights stand out to you from this situation?

Extra Insight

Because they had Greek names, the seven who were chosen may have come from the Greek-speaking believers who pointed out the discrimination. One source notes, "Although only a minority of Judean residents had Greek names, all *seven* of the new leaders have Greek names (Acts 6:5)."[3]

I noticed that:

- overlooking minority groups isn't a new concept;
- rumblings of discontent are part of church life, and how leadership handles them is key;
- equality and justice must be addressed but shouldn't take center stage; and
- the teaching of God's Word (message) and prayer take priority.

The Greek-speaking believers were likely Jews who spoke only Greek.[4] This labeled them as Hellenists, who also followed Greek customs and might have been immigrants who had returned to Palestine after being cast out of other parts of the Roman Empire.[5] The Hebrew-speaking Jews had prioritized their widows over the smaller number of Greek-speaking Jews, who differed from them in language and culture.

The apostles didn't ignore the plight of the downtrodden. They acted swiftly but were careful not to allow community needs to overtake the teaching of God's message and prayer.

What can we learn from the early church when it comes to balancing the teaching of God's Word with addressing issues of justice and practical needs?

We find hope in knowing that the early church preached the message and worked to ensure fair treatment and tangible help for the poor. If the early church could find the balance, so can we. Change begins one person at a time.

How can you care for someone's need in a practical way today?

How might you prioritize the studying or teaching of God's Word in your life today?

Today, we can listen to a sermon, podcast, or radio program. We could read a book, devotional, or the Scriptures themselves. When we study God's Word, it rarely goes unopposed. We have an enemy who doesn't like it when God's messages go forth and believers grow spiritually and increase in numbers.

Read Acts 6:8-15 and summarize what happened to Stephen in your own words below:

In the first half of today's chapter, we saw internal forces threaten the message of God, but now we see external opposition. The forces of deception heightened as more people awakened to God's message. Stephen was one of the men listed in the group of seven who would oversee the distribution of food to needy widows.

It is interesting that the concocted accusation against Stephen was that he was speaking against the Temple. One commentator explains that this was the most magnificent temple in the Mediterranean world and central to Jerusalem's economy.[7] To blaspheme against the Temple was to insult Jewish heritage, including the prophets and God's past messages. This calculated lie would strike at the heart of what the Jews sought to protect: their national identity. Those trying to oppose the gospel message used their understanding of culture to deceive.

It's still true today. When people awaken to God's powerful message, both internal and external forces seek to extinguish the flames of enthusiasm.

Extra Insight

The Greek word *stephanos* means "victor's crown." The other Greek word for crown, *diadema*, can be inherited, but the only way to get a *stephanos* is to earn it.[6]

What is an example of opposition to the gospel from outside the church that you have noticed recently?

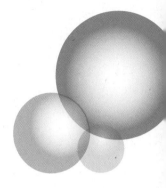

What are practical ways that we Christians can respectfully face opposition?

As we continue Stephen's story in tomorrow's lesson, we will find that speaking out boldly and respectfully rather than hiding the truth may be necessary at times. I'm glad that God gives us the power and wisdom needed to stand up for His truth against the internal and external forces that threaten us today.

Daily Wrap-Up

What is one way you noticed God at work in Acts 6?

How did the believers respond?

The Lord guided the church leadership to address problems within the church, and He allowed false charges against Stephen. The people focused on teaching and prayer as well as set a program in place to meet physical needs.

Today we focused on this truth: *internal and external forces threaten God's message, so we must prioritize the teaching of God's Word.*

How would you summarize your personal takeaway from today's lesson?

We shouldn't be shocked when we encounter rumblings of discontent within the church or when those outside the church make up lies to discredit the work of God. We have an enemy whose purpose is to steal, kill, and destroy, but Jesus came to give us life (John 10:10). That abundant life requires us to prioritize the teaching of God's Word and prayer so that we can realign ourselves continually to truth. Otherwise, we might find ourselves rewriting the script on the most important story ever told. We need grace, but we also must value truth—God's truth as found in His Word.

Talk with God

Lord, I need Your wisdom. Help me understand Your Word and how to apply Your message in the world today. Give me a passion for caring for others who have been treated unfairly or neglected, and give me passion for studying Your truth. I want to know You. Awaken me to You today! Amen.

Memory Verse Exercise

Read the Memory Verse on page 44 several times, and then fill in the blanks below as you recite it:

And _____ day, in the _____ and from house to _____, they continued to teach and _____ this message: "Jesus is the _____."

(Acts 5:42)

Day 3: Context for the Message

Scripture Focus

Acts 7

Big Idea

Knowing the backstory gives us context to understand God's message more fully.

We've talked this week about awakening to God's message, noting both the singularity and priority of God's message regarding Christ. Jesus was crucified and rose again in order to reconcile people to God through His blood. The early church focused intently on reaching others with the message that sinful people can draw near to a sinless God because of the sacrifice Jesus made on the cross.

This good news angered some Jews who did not believe this message and were losing the crowd's attention. They believed in a Messiah, but they didn't believe Jesus was God's anointed one.

Yesterday we met a man named Stephen who helped oversee the food program for widows in the burgeoning church. He also performed miracles that drew a crowd. Those who were jealous falsely accused him of blaspheming God by speaking against the Temple. Today we will hear in Stephen's own words the seamless story of God's plan that prepared the world for His Son's ultimate sacrifice. Stephen testified to his knowledge of the Scriptures, giving context for how Jesus fulfilled prophecies of the Old Testament.

Can you think of a time when hearing a backstory helped shift the way you thought or felt about something? If so, write below a few details of the situation:

At times I have enforced consequences for my children's actions without listening to their explanation of why they made a certain decision. If I had taken the time to hear the entire story, I might have chosen differently. Understanding the context of behaviors and events can cause a paradigm shift in our views. Today's chapter is long, but let's remember that Stephen sought to provide his audience with necessary context so that they might see the truth of the message that Jesus is the fulfillment of the promised Messiah.

Read Acts 7:1-38 and complete the summaries in the chart below to help us zoom out and see the larger picture of God's interactions with His people. I have written a few of them for you.

Person/ Place	Verses in Acts 7	Summary of what happened
1. Abraham	2-4	
2. Abraham	8	God instructed Abraham to circumcise his sons as a sign of covenant.
3. Joseph	9-14	
4. Moses	17-22	The Israelites greatly increased in number in Egypt and then were enslaved. Moses was born during this time.
5. Moses	23-29	
6. Moses	30-34	God appeared to Moses in a burning bush and sent him back to Egypt to free God's people.
7. Moses	35-38	

Answers on page 56.

Stephen then took a breath to make some application. He said, "Moses received life-giving words to pass on to us" (Acts 7:38b). Stephen wanted his audience to know that Moses spoke about Jesus as the fulfillment of God's message of life.

Has anything stood out to you so far in Stephen's background story? Jot down anything that has surprised you, reminded you of something, or caused you to pause and reread:

Extra Insight

"Stephen's manner of argument with its long historical recital may strike us as strange. But it has precedents in the similar recitals of history in the Old Testament" (Psalms 78; 105; 106).[8]

The lying witnesses said, "This man is always speaking against the holy Temple and against the law of Moses."

(Acts 6:13)

As I read Stephen's defense, I wondered why he spent so much time reviewing history rather than refuting the accusations leveled against him. Yet he knew his audience well. They revered the patriarchs and their Jewish history but were repeating their ancestors' mistakes and, consequently, missing God's promised Messiah.

After the historical review, Stephen continued his monologue, moving from a factual tone to one of indictment. Here is a summary of the text in Acts 7:37-48:

- The Israelites refused to listen to Moses and worshipped idols instead (vv. 39-42).
- They carried the Tabernacle through the wilderness and brought it into the Promised Land years later under the leadership of Joshua (vv. 44-45).
- King David found favor with God and asked to build a permanent temple, but it was actually Solomon who carried out the construction (vv. 46-47).

Read Acts 7:48-50, most of which is quoted from the prophet Isaiah (66:1-2), and write below how these verses relate to the charge directed against Stephen in Acts 6:13 (see the margin).

Stephen didn't respond directly to the charges made against him, but he wanted everyone to know that serving God had never been about a place or a building. (He did not speak against the Temple, by the way.) He began his monologue by citing that God called Abraham from Mesopotamia, intentionally reminding the crowd that God rules over all the earth, not just the nation of Israel. In fact, he was passionate about their shortsightedness.

Read Acts 7:51-59 and label the following statements with *S* for Stephen or *J* for the Jewish leaders:

1. _____ **Believed God's message so zealously that he lived it, taught it, and explained the context behind it.**

2. _____ **Repeated the mistakes that the Israelites had made for generations by valuing human strength (trusting in idols, temples, and false gods) more than divine dependence.**

3. _____ **Desired popularity more than truth and went to great lengths to quell any opposition to their popular status.**

The Jewish leaders covered not only their physical ears but also their spiritual ears, refusing to hear the truth of God's message. This leads us to consider these questions about our own lives:

- When have we valued human strength more than divine dependence?
- Are we studying God's message in context and passionately embracing it?
- Do we cower when others oppose our beliefs, or do we stand boldly for truth?

I wonder how Stephen would be criticized today for his harsh words of indictment. We should never be cutting and mean-spirited with our words, but neither should we avoid speaking the truth when it's difficult. Sometimes truth cuts deep, convicting us of sin and turning us toward the Lord.

We need to ask ourselves if we'd rather hear comforting lies or painful truth. Stephen's commitment to truth caused him physical pain. While we might not be in danger of being stoned, I believe God wants to awaken us to greater passion for sharing and defending His gospel message—always with a heart of love.

I want more passion for God's message in my daily experience. Sometimes I excuse my indifference toward sharing the gospel because I don't want to seem pushy or rude or make assumptions. Though it's important not to shove our beliefs down people's throats, I wonder if, collectively speaking, we have lost our fervor for God's truth.

Extra Insight

Some seeming contradictions between Stephen's message and the Old Testament regarding the number in Jacob's family and his burial site can be explained by Stephen's use of the Septuagint (LXX)—the Greek translation of the Old Testament.[9]

Extra Insight

Stephen's vision of Jesus standing at the right hand of God incited the crowd to mob violence, causing them to disregard their own laws for legal execution.[10]

Let's end our lesson today by stoking the embers of our passion for God's message.

Pick one of the following two activities to complete as you consider your own response to Stephen's message.

1. **Write a personal prayer asking God to awaken in you a greater passion for the gospel message:**

2. **Identify and commit to study a subject on which you want to have more historical and biblical context and understanding (for example, evangelism, women in ministry, sexuality, financial management, the role of government, etc.).**

Daily Wrap-Up

In Acts 7, Stephen gives us a history lesson with many divine interventions and responses of the people. Choose just one activity of God and one response of His people that stood out to you in today's reading.

What is one way you noticed God at work in Acts 7?

How did the believers respond?

In our study of Acts, we will see God rescue some of His followers from death. Yet here God did not step in to save Stephen from stoning. Even when he knew the outcome would not be physical deliverance, Stephen still prayed for his accusers. This reveals the power of God to make us more like Jesus. Stephen's words echo those of Jesus on the cross. "Father, forgive them, for they don't know what they are doing" (Luke 23:34a).

Today we focused on this truth: *knowing the backstory gives us context to understand God's message more fully.*

How would you summarize your personal takeaway from today's lesson?

I want to awaken more and more to God's message and to people's stories so that I respond to others with compassion. Stephen demonstrated that we can change our posture toward those who oppose us. His life ended with prayers of grace for the stone-throwers attacking him. Awakening to God's message can make that possible in our lives too!

Talk with God

Lord, there is so much I don't understand. Give me context through the Holy Spirit to read Your Word with understanding. Help me to trust You and forgive others. Your message leads to life. Help me to depend on You and believe Your truth rather than make up my own according to my logic or emotions. Awaken me to You today! Amen.

Memory Verse Exercise

Read the Memory Verse on page 44 several times, and then fill in the blanks below as you recite it:

And _____ day, in the _____ and from _____ to _____, they continued to teach and _____ this _____: "Jesus is the _____."

(Acts 5:42)

Day 4: Personal Messages

When my son was seven years old, I asked him what he wanted to do when he grew up. He said he would travel around telling people about Jesus. At this tender age, he was surrounded by the message of Christ at both school and church. Because his father was a pastor, he had double doses of Sunday school during both morning services in addition to a midweek children's program.

I was envisioning crowds gathering to listen to my son preach in Billy Graham–fashion until he added that he also would feed the people lunch. When I questioned how he would accomplish this, he explained that he planned to tell people about Jesus one at a time, possibly traveling in a trailer where he would sleep and invite each person he talked with to have a sandwich. I smiled at his endearing plan that reminded me of God's love for individuals.

Scripture Focus

Acts 8

Big Idea

We can share the message with one person at a time, leaving the results to the Lord.

So far in the Book of Acts, we've seen the message about Christ proclaimed to crowds by the apostles and by the first Christian martyr, Stephen. Today we will see the individual nature of God's pursuit of people and discover how the message spread more rapidly during a season of persecution.

If you are a follower of Jesus, where were you when you first responded to God's invitation—in a crowd, in a small group, with one person, or alone?

I was in a small group when my Sunday school teacher explained the gospel in a way that evoked a response in me. My belief was limited and immature at my young age, but I'm grateful that humble faith in God's message about Christ is all it takes to begin a relationship with Him. My faith grew over time, but I still appreciate the simplicity of the gospel message, which even a child can embrace and desire to share with others.

Before we jump into Acts 8, take a moment to review Acts 1:8 in the margin, and underline the word *Samaria*.

The words of Acts 1:8 will unfold before our very eyes as the gospel spreads to Samaria and makes its way to the ends of the earth.

Read Acts 8:1-3 and describe what happened as a result of Stephen's death:

Extra Insight

"The Samaritans were a mixed race with a pagan core." They were considered half-breeds because they were "descendants of the colonists brought in by the king of Assyria" who intermarried with Jews in the surrounding areas.[11]

Saul, along with other leaders, began to hunt for Christ-followers with the intent to imprison them. This scattered the believers, but it did not close their mouths.

Read Acts 8:4-25. Then write the name of the person or place described in each statement below:

Philip went to this city to tell people about the gospel. It wasn't a Gentile nation, but Jews generally hated these fellow Israelites who had intermarried with outsiders such as the Assyrians. The hostility was mutual, but the crowds were eager to hear the message that was accompanied by miraculous signs. (vv. 4-8)

_____

This guy was one of the seven men who had been appointed to oversee the food distribution to widows alongside Stephen, and he preached that Jesus was the Messiah in Samaria. (v. 5)

_____

This man had been a sorcerer referred to as the Great One because he did magic. After he believed the message about Christ and was baptized, he wanted to buy the power to bestow God's Spirit onto people. Peter rebuked him for desiring God's power with wrong motives. (vv. 13, 18-20)

_____

This man was sent to Samaria with the apostle John after the disciples heard how the gospel was spreading there. When he and John laid hands on the new believers, they received the Holy Spirit. He admonished Simon the sorcerer for trying to purchase the power of God. (vv. 14, 17, 21)

_____

I noticed a few key principles in this passage. First, persecution forced the gospel to spread beyond the church's holy huddle. Second, people have always been tempted to desire the power and privileges of God's message for their own personal gain. And finally, faith comes by hearing God's Word, so we must continue to present it even in the midst of opposition.

How have you experienced any kind of "persecution" or discrimination when it comes to your faith?

I was teased a little in high school because of my faith, and I've encountered people who compete for personal prestige rather than advocate kingdom comradery; but I've never had to move, endure physical pain or threats, or face legal trouble because of my faith in Christ. It seems likely that there is a connection between the lack of persecution and lack of spiritual awakening in Western Christianity. Studying Acts reminds us of the power of God's message in the midst of persecution.

What is something the early Christians did not stop doing despite persecution?

What would motivate you to continue doing this even if you were to suffer persecution?

The disciples kept preaching wherever they went. We don't necessarily want to invite persecution, but we can prepare for it by boldly praying and sharing God's message—whether it is welcome, forbidden, or diluted in our culture. We can awaken anew to the truth that the message about Jesus is the only message that really matters for all eternity. The early Christians were able to keep praying and sharing the gospel through the power of the Holy Spirit.

Did Acts 8:14-17 bring up any new questions regarding the Holy Spirit for you? If so, write them below:

I questioned why the Spirit didn't immediately come upon the Samaritans when they accepted God's message. Instead, they received the Holy Spirit after Peter and John laid hands on them. These verses about the Holy Spirit might be some of the most controversial verses in the Book of Acts. They raise questions such as:

- Why was the gift of the Spirit delayed for the Samaritans?
- Is it necessary for an apostle (or pastor) to lay hands on new believers in order for them to receive the Holy Spirit?

In these situations, we must look for context. By looking at the book as a whole, we learn that:

- Peter said you must repent, be baptized, and then receive the Holy Spirit (Acts 2:38);
- Saul was filled with the Spirit before he was baptized (Acts 9:17); and
- the Gentiles received the Holy Spirit and were then baptized (Acts 10:44-47).

As the church was being established, the order of water and Spirit baptism varied. One possible reason the Samaritan believers did not receive the Holy Spirit until after Peter and John laid hands on them might have to do with apostolic testimony. The church in Jerusalem might have struggled to understand that Samaritans could be Spirit-filled believers. With the eyewitness testimony of Peter and John, the Jerusalem church would more readily incorporate the Samaritan believers into the community of faith.[12]

We should not read this passage as prescriptive but as descriptive. As we discover how the gospel spread from Jerusalem to Judea to Samaria, we see that God sometimes chose to delay the giving of His Spirit. We should guard against building a theological perspective on when and how we receive God's Spirit based on this chapter.

If this passage causes you to question whether or not you have received the Holy Spirit, I have good news for you. We are not living during the establishment of the church, a time when more and more non-Jews were believing in Christ for the first time and God was breaking through barriers to build the church. Just a couple of decades after the time of Acts 8, the apostle Paul would teach that we receive the Holy Spirit when we decide to follow Jesus. Ephesians 1:13 says, "And now you Gentiles have also heard the truth, the Good News that God saves you. And when you believed in Christ, he identified you as his own by giving you the Holy Spirit, whom he promised long ago." If you are a believer in Christ, you have the Holy Spirit living inside you.

Think back to when you first sensed the Holy Spirit at work in your life. It may not have been as demonstrative as what we read about in Acts. Consider times when you felt conviction for sin, nudges to serve, power to show kindness, or any other power that was sourced from the divine. Make a few notes below:

Now ask God to awaken you to His Spirit at work in your life today. Write a brief prayer below:

I want to continue awakening to the Spirit's leading in my life. Usually, I notice His hand in hindsight rather than in the moment. He has helped me to forgive, guided me in prayer, and inspired ideas when I thought I had none. This same Spirit led Philip in a new direction.

Philip had been preaching that Jesus was the Messiah to crowds, but then the Spirit turned him in a direction that wouldn't have made logical sense for a disciple on the move.

Extra Insight

"The term *eunuch* normally indicates a person who has been castrated....The term could also be used, however, to refer simply to a court official. This may be the sense here [in Acts 8:27]."[13]

Read Acts 8:26-40 and answer the following questions:

What kind of road did the angel of the Lord direct Philip down? (v. 26)

Whom did Philip meet on that road? (v. 27)

What book was the stranger reading? (v. 28)

What did the Holy Spirit instruct Philip to do? (v. 29)

In your opinion, what was the heart posture of the eunuch? (vv. 31-36)

What did the eunuch ask for Philip to do? (vv. 36-38)

What did the Spirit of the Lord do to Philip next? (v. 39)

God's angel directed Philip away from the crowds to an individual. He was now spreading the message the way my son thought he might do it—one person at a time. God had something big in mind. This eunuch worked for the queen of Ethiopia, which scholars believe is modern Sudan.[15] We will not know this side of heaven how this man's nation was impacted by his conversion on that desert road. He was seeking God, and the Lord used Philip to give him further understanding. This shows us that God's heart has always been for the nations. He supernaturally sent the message about Jesus to an entire nation through Philip.

Philip preached a consistent message, but each person had to decide how they would respond to it. Simon's fascination with the supernatural greatly contrasts the eunuch's hunger for truth. The disciples were entrusted to share the message with a focus on faithfulness, not results. They also united around the message. When the Spirit of God was moving, Peter and John came to cooperate, not compete. They didn't fight over sheep but focused on preaching and teaching the message. This stands out to me because persecution sometimes can be a catalyst for division. Times of difficulty in my life often propel me to turn inward, but the disciples focused outward. With a clarity of message and the power of the Holy Spirit guiding them, they saw many people awaken to God for the first time. You and I can share God's love in our own sphere of influences even through the challenging circumstances we sometimes face.

Daily Wrap-Up

What is one way you noticed God at work in Acts 8?

How did the believers respond?

Maybe you noticed that Philip responded to the Holy Spirit leading him away from the fawning crowds. Perhaps you learned from Simon to ask for a pure heart. The eunuch's thirst for God may have inspired you to seek God more actively. The Book of Acts awakens us to the work of God. We may not have experienced serious persecution, but our difficulties can become catalysts of growth, driving us toward God rather than away from Him.

Today we focused on this truth: *we can share the message with one person at a time, leaving the results to the Lord.*

How would you summarize your personal takeaway from today's lesson?

I was inspired by the eunuch to seek God with a whole heart and believe that He cares enough to meet me wherever I am. I'm smiling just knowing that God sees me and cares for me today. I hope you know that He sees you and cares for you too. He longs to awaken us to Him—one person at a time.

Talk with God

Lord, let change begin with me. May difficulties propel me toward You. Give me a heart that seeks You and searches for greater understanding. Lord, awaken me today so that I might share Your message with greater clarity and boldness. Amen.

Memory Verse Exercise

Read the Memory Verse on page 44 several times, and then fill in the blanks below as you recite it:

And _____ day, ____ the _____ and from _____ to _____, they _____ to teach and _____ this _____: "_____ is the _____."

(Acts 5:42)

Day 5: The Life-Changing Message

I love stories of those whose lives have been changed by God's gospel message. C. S. Lewis, one of my favorite authors, scoffed at Christianity until he embraced the gospel and wrote some of the most compelling works of fiction and nonfiction that illustrate God's grace. *A Life Observed* is the spiritual biography of his life. Similarly, *The Case for Christ* is a book, later adapted into a movie, that chronicles the story of an investigative reporter named Lee Strobel who set out to disapprove the Resurrection but came to believe in it instead. These stories move me, as does the story of a couple I met who were formerly Muslims from Pakistan whose lives were radically changed by Christ.

Have you been moved by a story of God's message changing the course of someone's life? If so, record a few details below:

In Acts 9, Luke records the conversion of one of the book's main characters. We met him briefly in Acts 8:1 as Saul, who witnessed and silently condoned the killing of Stephen. If we were taking his spiritual temperature in terms of his openness to the gospel of Jesus at that point, I'm not sure it would register on the thermometer at all.

Read Acts 9:1-19 and answer the following questions:

What was Saul's initial posture toward Christ-followers? (vv. 1-2)

What happened to change Saul's opinion? (vv. 3-9)

What did God command Ananias to do, and what were his objections? (vv. 11-14)

What two things did the Lord reveal to Ananias about Saul? (vv. 15-16)

Extra Insight

Luke recorded the account of Saul's conversion three separate times in Acts 9; 22; and 26.

"'The Way' is probably the earliest self-designation of the followers of Jesus, the earliest term for the church."[16]

What did Saul do immediately after his sight returned—even before eating? (vv. 18-19)

Of all the details in this account, what stands out to you about Saul's conversion?

I noticed that God intervened supernaturally but also used another believer to help open Saul's eyes in both a physical and spiritual sense. The event seems glamorous as we read of bright lights and God's audible voice. Yet as one source points out, Saul goes from self-confident independence to childlike dependence as he becomes an instrument in God's hands who will suffer much in his new faith (vv. 15-16).[17]

To believe in Christ's message means surrendering our wills so that our lives become instruments in God's hands. While we may not see a bright light or hear an audible voice, we move from darkness to light by believing in Christ.

How has God used other believers as His instrument to encourage, strengthen, or share God's message with you? Record a few examples:

Extra Insight

Acts 9:15 refers to Saul as a chosen "instrument" of God. "The noun 'instrument' is used elsewhere in Luke-Acts with the literal meaning of a container or vessel (10:11, 16; 27:17; Luke 8:16; 17:31)."[18]

When has the Lord used you as His instrument to encourage, strengthen, or share God's message with others? Record a few examples:

You may have a dynamic story like Saul's, or you may not know exactly when you crossed the threshold of faith. Perhaps all you know is that once you were in darkness and now you see clearly that Christ is the hope of the world. I have only vague memories of when I first believed. I remember my Sunday school teacher talking with me about Jesus and my baptism when I was nine years old. However, Christian mentors, Bible study, challenges, and time have grown my faith and given me direction in life.

I heard someone once say that mess + age = message. We all wrestle with the mess of sin and difficult circumstances over time. Saul had plenty of mess in his hunt to persecute Christians. We may not have persecuted Christians, but even as a nine-year-old girl I knew my bent toward sin was more than I could manage. We need God! We are a mess without Him. With age, God sanctifies and equips us to share His message. He calls us to be His instruments, and sometimes this involves suffering.

After his conversion, Saul didn't yet have much "age" or experience as a Christ-follower to add to his mess but that didn't hold him back from boldly sharing the gospel message.

Read Acts 9:20-31 and note below a few of the words used in these verses to describe Saul's ministry (preaching and teaching):

v. 20

v. 22

v. 28

v. 29

Now summarize in your own words the state of the church described in verse 31:

The church experienced peace even in the midst of persecution, becoming stronger and bigger as believers lived in the fear of the Lord and the encouragement of the Holy Spirit.

Do you think these things could be said about the universal church today? Why or why not?

You and I are part of the church today. The message that changed Saul's life continues to change ours as well.

What are some tangible ways we can attune more intentionally to the fear of the Lord and the encouragement of the Holy Spirit?

For me, it often comes back to the Word of God. Through reading and studying the Bible, I connect with God and find peace and strength as I realign to the reality that He is God and I am not. I also sense the Holy Spirit encouraging me through the truths in Scripture and the ways they speak into my daily life. Reading about men like Saul, who once was passionately against God and then directed that energy toward spreading God's message, inspires me.

The Lord took Saul's previously misguided passion and turned it around so that he preached boldly about Christ. And God does the same thing in our lives.

Can you identify any inclinations or passions you possessed before you believed in Christ that God has redeemed for His use (personality traits, talents, resources, hobbies, and so forth.)? If something comes to mind, write it below:

I was young when I first believed in Jesus, but even before that decision, I had the desire to study and understand concepts. God has channeled this interest of mine toward writing Bible studies that help others to understand God's message. You may possess musical talents, humor, or Saul-like passion that can be used to share God's message with others. While Saul was still a young believer, he was well versed in the Hebrew Scriptures. When the message about Jesus clicked for him, he had a clear and passionate understanding that the Messiah had come. Though at first he wasn't accepted by other believers, in time he proved his sincerity.

As you think about your mess + age, how do you feel uniquely called to share God's love with others?

Junior high proved to be a difficult season for me, and my own children struggled through those years as well. As a result, I feel called to serve students in this age group through my mess + age. Maybe your story includes infertility, singleness, parenting difficult children, health challenges, or misplaced zeal. God won't waste a bit of what you've endured but will use your story to help others. Regardless of where we seek to share God's message, Saul serves as an example for us of how God can redirect our mess into a vehicle for His message.

Let's recap what we've learned from Saul's story:

- God uses unlikely people to deliver His messages.

- Our mess + age becomes our message.

- When we truly encounter the living God, our lives are never the same.

- Other: _____

Put a star next to the truth that most resonates with you today.

The last section of Acts 9 reminds us through the example of Peter's ministry that God works simultaneously in our lives and the lives of others.

Read Acts 9:32-43 and briefly describe one of the two miracles performed:

Through Peter, God healed a paralyzed man and raised a woman from the dead. In both Lydda and Joppa, word of God's healing power spread, and many believed in Jesus. These verses at the end of Saul's incredible transformation story remind us that the life-changing gospel message spreads as a variety of people engage the message in a variety of ways.

It's so easy to become shortsighted and think that God works with others only in the way He works in our lives. The message remains the same: Jesus died for our sin to reconcile us to God. But the methods and modes of how we share that message can look very different. As Saul awakened to the truth about Jesus, his life was forever changed. Certainly, if we could sit with Aeneas and Tabitha (Dorcas), they would concur that knowing Jesus brings life-change. Just as the power of God allowed Aeneas to walk and Tabitha to breathe again, this same life-changing power is available to us through faith. I hope you experience this power in your life personally today!

Daily Wrap-Up

What is one way you noticed God at work in Acts 9?

How did the believers respond?

Saul awakened to the truth when He encountered the living God. He prayed, prepared, and preached. The gospel message changes the course of our lives as well.

Today we focused on this truth: *awakening to God's message changes the course of our lives.*

How would you summarize your personal takeaway from today's lesson?

If we slow down and reflect, we'll find that our lives have never really been the same since we believed in Jesus. Our lives haven't always been easy, but they have been transformed. I'm asking God to awaken in me a greater thirst for Him. I don't want to be satisfied with half-heartedness. I desire to see the Lord move in big ways, even if it includes suffering. Let's continue to bring our messes to God each day so that He can use us as His messengers to tell more people that life change is possible through Christ.

Talk with God

Lord, here is my mess. Please use it to shape Your message in me. Give me a healthy fear of You and the encouragement of the Holy Spirit. If You could use Saul, who once perse-cuted Your followers, I know You can use me. Guide me to share Your message with clarity and direction. Thank You for sending Your Son for me. Awaken me to the power of Your message and Spirit today. Amen.

Memory Verse Exercise

Read the Memory Verse on page 44 several times, and then fill in the blanks below as you recite it:

_____ _____ _____, ____ the _____ and _____
_____ to _____, they _____ to _____
and _____ this _____: "_____ is the
_____."

(Acts 5:42)

Weekly Wrap-Up

Review the Big Idea for each day, and then write any personal application that comes to mind.

Day 1: The Message of Life

Big Idea: we want to awaken to God's message because it's the only one that really matters.

Personal Application:_____

_____

Day 2: The Priority of the Message

Big Idea: internal and external forces threaten God's message, so we must prioritize the teaching of God's Word.

Personal Application:_____

_____

Day 3: Context for the Message

Big Idea: knowing the backstory gives us context to understand God's message more fully.

Personal Application:_____

_____

Day 4: Personal Messages

Big Idea: we can share the message with one person at a time, leaving the results to the Lord.

Personal Application:_____

_____

Day 5: The Life-Changing Message

Big Idea: awakening to God's message changes the course of our lives.

Personal Application:_____

_____

Video Viewer Guide: Week 2

Acts 5:29-32, 42

Awakening to _____ _____ usually includes some level of mess.

_____ + _____ = Message

Acts 6:1

Awakening to _____ _____, results in _____.

Awakening to _____ _____ means we are able to _____

____ _____.

Acts 7:51-60

God doesn't want a _____, he wants _____ _____.

Week 3

Awakening to God's Freedom

Acts 10–14

Memory Verse

Then Peter replied, "I see very clearly that God shows no favoritism. In every nation he accepts those who fear him and do what is right. This is the message of Good News for the people of Israel—that there is peace with God through Jesus Christ, who is Lord of all."

(Acts 10:34-36)

Day 1: Freedom from Favoritism

My daughter described how the lunchroom scenario had changed radically when she entered junior high. In elementary school, students ate at small tables with whichever classmates they happened to walk beside when leaving class. But in junior high, the cafeteria had long tables packed with kids who had attended different elementary schools, and the table groupings made clear statements about shared identity. A few of her friends had special diets, and they congregated at one table. Some groups were students who excelled in academics and others were athletes who played together on sports teams. She also described the table where the "popular" kids sat. They had name-brand clothes, inside jokes, and a sense of belonging she envied.

Whether you had a similar or different experience in junior high or middle school, can you think of a time when a certain group had special qualities or rules, allowing only certain people to be included? If something comes to mind, write it below:

Big Idea

As we awaken to see people the way God does, we can cross the boundaries of difference and find freedom from favoritism.

I can recall scenes from my own teenage years that are similar to what my daughter described, but I also have encountered exclusive cliques in churches, neighborhood organizations, and school meetings. As we dig into the text this week, our focus will be awakening to God's freedom. We'll observe the tension that resulted when a unique community that was embracing their age-old traditions collided with God's inclusive gospel that invites all to believe.

God chose the Jewish nation and blessed them. He used them to share the message about His love, the separation we experience as a result of sin, and the hope of restoration through a Messiah. God's heart never has been exclusive, as we discover from Old Testament stories of men and women from other nations who embraced God's message. In his Gospel, Luke records the words of Jesus regarding a widow from Zarephath and Naaman the Syrian, two Old Testament examples of God intervening in the lives of those outside the Jewish community (Luke 4:23-27). As a Gentile himself, Luke also chronicles the Samaritans' exposure to the gospel and the salvation of an Ethiopian official (Acts 8). Today we will see a definitive change unfold among the Jewish believers as the message of freedom in Christ reaches even more Gentiles.

Extra Insight

Caesarea was Judea's second-largest city after Jerusalem and boasted a large Gentile population whose patron deity was the goddess Fortune.[1]

Read Acts 10:1-16 and either draw or describe the two visions in the clouds below:

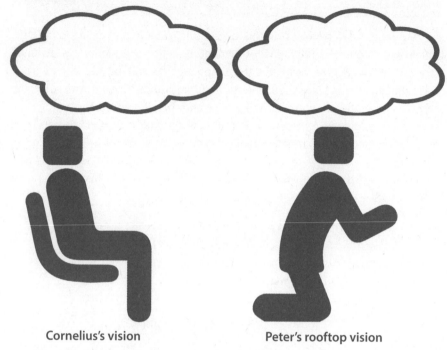

Cornelius's vision   Peter's rooftop vision

What do Cornelius and Peter have in common?

How are they different?

Extra Insight

Peter's protest against eating unclean food parallels Ezekiel's response to God in (Ezekiel 4:14). The basic dietary laws in Leviticus 11 were widely practiced by all Jews at that time, whether they were devout or nominal in religious practice.[2]

Both men saw visions, feared God, prayed regularly, and served God in practical ways. God called them both by name. Yet Cornelius was an uncircumcised Gentile as well as a Roman centurion assigned to an Italian regiment of soldiers living in Caesarea. Luke described him as devout and God-fearing, but these qualities were most often applied to "gentile sympathizers who were not yet full converts to Judaism."[3] Peter wasn't the strictest observer of Jewish law as he was staying at the home of a tanner, which rabbis considered an unclean trade.[4] However, he was a Jew. Jews lived by the law of Moses, which called them to eat, live, and interact very differently from Romans. As we read these visions, we need to understand Jewish culture. To our modern mindset, Cornelius inviting a Jewish man to his home or Peter having a vision in which he was instructed to eat unclean food may not seem very radical.

Read Acts 10:17-33. What clues in the text alert us to the cultural barriers Peter is crossing?

We like to surround ourselves with like-minded people. Junior high lunch tables and our own friendship preferences often reveal this truth. We are naturally drawn to those who look like us, think like us, and share our spiritual beliefs. The messages of our culture include showing tolerance, appreciating diversity, and listening to learn, but this was not the case in the culture of the original audience of Luke's account. Perhaps these insights will help us understand how unprecedented the interaction of Peter and Cornelius truly was:

- From a Judean's perspective, a Roman centurion represented the occupying power that oppressed their people. From a Christian's perspective, Rome was responsible for the crucifixion of Christ.[5]
- Normal Jewish hospitality included meals and lodging, but strict Judeans would not have hosted Gentiles, who were considered impure. Peter invited the messengers to stay the night.[6]
- Entering a Gentile home would have rendered Peter ceremonially unclean and was forbidden by Jewish law.[7]

At the time of these two visions, which occurred ten years after Pentecost, most converts to Christianity were Jews.[8] These converts were comfortable sharing their new faith with people of similar backgrounds, cultural norms, and family rules.

To bring Gentiles fully into the Christian experience would upset everything from how people should wash their hands before dinner to what would be allowed on the menu. Rome had imposed the Pax Romana ("Roman peace" that lasted about two centuries), during which time Jews and Gentiles lived peaceably in Caesarea's divided population. But God was offering peace through Christ rather than government enforcement.[9]

Breaking these barriers required divine intervention. I wish I could have been a fly on the wall at the dinner table at Simon the tanner's house on the evening of Peter's vision. I would have loved to hear the conversations as they processed the dual visions and the implications for Christianity. We discover some of Peter's conclusions through the words he spoke in Cornelius's home.

Read Acts 10:34-48, and write below the statement Peter makes in verse 34:

"The wording of verse 36 incorporates allusions to two Old Testament texts, Psalm 107:20, 'He *sent forth* his *word* and *healed* them,' and Isaiah 52:7, 'the feet of him *who brings good tidings*, who publishes *peace*.'"[10]

According to verse 35, whom does God accept?

In verse 36, what does Peter say about how people find peace with God?

According to verse 43, who will have their sins forgiven?

What parts of Peter's message would have helped to unify Jews and Gentiles?

Though the culture in which Cornelius and Peter lived was different from ours, Peter's message resounds into our world today with just as much relevance. Then and now, the gospel bridges the gap between race, culture, and historical divides. It has the power to unify us as we awaken to the Holy Spirit of God. Our sin causes us to experience separation from God, but through Christ we find freedom and peace with God.

It's important to note that the peace referenced in Acts 10:36 is more than a state of calmness. One commentator writes, "Peace is used here in its full sense as a synonym for 'salvation' . . . and denotes not merely the absence of strife and enmity between man and God but also the positive blessings that develop in a state of reconciliation."[11] Though the Jewish law was meant to be a tutor for God's people while they waited for the Messiah (Galatians 3:24), God showed Peter that the law also could be a wall limiting Christ's message rather than showing all people their need for a Savior. We don't want anything to become a hindrance to the peace God offers us—whether it's the law or something else that divides us.

Awakening to freedom from favoritism is messy. When we begin to "sit at a different lunch table," we might discover that some things we held as law actually are preferences. It's also possible that we will find a new perspective, begin to appreciate differences, and learn to love even when we disagree.

The apostle Paul's letters to the New Testament churches are full of examples of the struggle to live out unity in the midst of real-life differences. We need to acknowledge the natural discord that accompanies differences but also the truth that God doesn't show favoritism. As we awaken to see people the way

God does, we can cross the boundaries of difference and find freedom from favoritism.

How might the Lord be calling you to change your thinking or actions after reading Acts 10?

Reading Peter's words reminds me to keep the main thing the main thing in conversations about controversial matters. He didn't list how Gentiles needed to conform to Judaism's standards in order to enter the faith. He focused on the gospel—the good news about Christ. I'm asking the Lord to help me steer my comments toward faith in Jesus, knowing that divine intervention is still needed to bridge the gaps that divide us today. As you interact with others this week, look for opportunities to find common ground and spread God's love in our divided world.

Daily Wrap-Up

What is one way you noticed God at work in Acts 10?

How did the believers respond?

God worked through simultaneous visions to a Jew and a Gentile. His intervention sparked conversations that led to inclusion rather than exclusion. Peter initially protested in the face of change, but he couldn't ignore God's message.

Today we focused on this truth: *as we awaken to see people the way God does, we can cross the boundaries of difference and find freedom from favoritism.*

How would you summarize your personal takeaway from today's lesson?

We can awaken to God in everyday life as we remember that He welcomes all who would believe in His Son. Freedom comes when we see people the way God does and ask Him to awaken us to His love for them.

Talk with God

Lord, I need Your wisdom to sort out differences. Give me ears to listen to others and, above all, to You. Help me to view people and circumstances with Your perspective. Awaken me to see where rules have built walls in my relationships, and bring the freedom that only You can! Help me to be free from favoritism so that I can share your message of peace through Christ. Amen.

Memory Verse Exercise

Read the Memory Verse on page 74 several times, and then fill in the blanks below as you recite it:

Then _____ replied, "I see very clearly that God shows no
_____. In every nation he _____ those who
fear him and do what is right. This is the message of Good News for the
people of _____—that there is peace with God through Jesus
Christ, who is Lord of all."

(Acts 10:34-36)

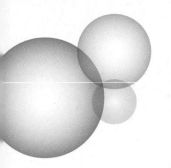

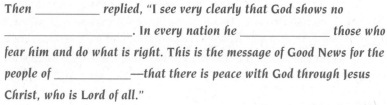

Day 2: Freedom from Tradition

Scripture Focus

Acts 11

Big Idea

Determining essentials helps us enjoy traditions rather than become enslaved by them.

Whenever our family gathers around the dinner table, we each share a high and low point from our day. We've done this for years, and our kids loved it when they were little. Only one of our four children currently lives at home, so meals around the table have become rare. One day my daughter invited a boy she likes to join us for Sunday lunch, and she shot me an alarmed look when I asked who was going first with highs and lows. Our tradition was fine when it was just us, but she thought he might find it uncomfortable.

For those of us who practice them, traditions can forge routines, memories, and common bonds. For others, those same traditions can seem strange or unfamiliar.

What are some traditions you observed growing up or have implemented in your own family?

Maybe you always cut your own Christmas tree or dressed up for Easter Sunday. Many of our traditions are preferences that provide structure and belonging. For the Jewish people, traditions were closely linked to laws given by God.

Jews who believed that Jesus was the promised Messiah still held to their Jewish customs and laws. Christianity did not eradicate the celebration of Jewish holy days such as Passover, but the inclusion of the Gentiles mandated a delineation of *requirements* versus *nonessentials* for new believers. Requirements were practices that applied to every Christian, while nonessentials were areas where difference and individual freedom were permissible. Though the Jewish law was interwoven into the fabric of early Christianity, Jewish believers learned that God did not want them to force their traditions on the wider group of Gentiles who would believe in Christ.

Similarly, we need to awaken to freedom regarding nonessentials today. Sharing highs and lows at the dinner table, for example, is not a religious observance but only a tradition that enhances our family conversation. We would not propose that all families need to follow *our* way to have good conversation at dinner. This distinction between essential practice and personal preference is as important today as it was in the early church. The church's awakening to freedom from tradition reminds us to guard against mandating our preferences to other believers. God's Word guides us in this pursuit.

Read Acts 11:1-18 and describe what helped change the minds of the believers about including Gentiles:

The church members were astonished that Peter would break the law, but they listened to his story. When he described the Holy Spirit falling on the Gentiles as He fell on them in the beginning, they stopped objecting and started praising God. They were convinced that the Gentiles had been given the privilege of repenting of sin and receiving eternal life through Christ just as they had been.

When trying to sort out essentials and nonessentials, we can learn to listen with openness and ask questions. God works outside of the boxes we sometimes put Him in.

What has helped you to discern the difference between *requirements* and *preferences* in following Jesus?

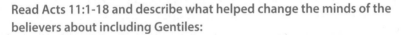

The gals in the pilot group discussed this question at length. We all agreed that when it comes to "requirements" for Christians, the only one is faith. We can make a list of many other good things that Scripture encourages us to do such as pray, fellowship, serve, and study God's Word. Yet the difference between a Christ-follower and a nonbeliever comes down to faith alone. Areas of preference would include things such as methods of baptism and Communion, worship formats, music styles, prayer practices, and approaches to Bible study.

Here are some principles we see the early believers employ in Acts 11 to discern between requirements and preferences:

1. Consider the source.
   They were listening to Peter, whom Christ said would be given the keys to the kingdom (Matthew 16:19).
2. Listen to the full story.
   They learned about Peter's and Cornelius's visions and the evidence of the Holy Spirit falling on the Gentiles at their conversion.
3. Be willing to change your opinion.
   Their criticism turned to agreement and praising God.

The early church sets an example we can follow. We don't want to be easily swayed from foundational beliefs, but when it comes to understanding changes or differences, we can learn to discern. Perhaps we engage in research, consult a mentor, or process our views in a journal. We want to hold unswervingly to our essential gospel beliefs without missing God's leading in gray areas because of shortsightedness.

The remaining verses of Acts 11 tell us what happened after the Jewish believers embraced the Gentiles and encouraged them.

Read Acts 11:19-30, and circle the letter of the correct ending for each statement:

1. (Verse 19) At first, the believers who were scattered because of persecution traveled to Phoenicia, Cyprus, and Antioch and preached to:

A. Gentiles,
B. only Syrians, or
C. only Jews.

2. (Verses 20-21) Some of the believers in Antioch began preaching to the Gentiles (Greeks), and the response was:

A. a large number of Gentiles believed,
B. no one believed, or
C. a few Gentiles believed.

3. (Verse 26) In Antioch, the believers were first called:

A. the Way,
B. Christians, or
C. Jesus people.

4. (Verses 22-26) Barnabas was Saul's ministry partner who:

    A. was sent to Antioch by the Jerusalem church,

    B. encouraged the believers in Antioch to stay true to the Lord,

    C. was full of the Holy Spirit and strong in faith,

    D. looked for Saul and brought him back to Antioch,

    E. stayed in Antioch for a year with Saul teaching, or

    F. all of the above.

5. (Verses 27-30) After a prophet came to Antioch and predicted a severe famine, the believers there

    A. collected money to provide help for their brothers and sisters in Judea,

    B. decided there was nothing they could do, or

    C. asked Barnabas and Saul to tell them what to do.

Through Peter's and Cornelius's visions, God helped the Jewish believers discern that God accepted Gentiles without the trappings of Judaism, and the Jewish believers embraced the Gentiles. Over time, many Gentiles believed in Jesus, as happened specifically in Antioch. Barnabas and Saul spent a year teaching and discipling these new believers. Through dependence on the Holy Spirit, a man predicted a coming famine so that the believers at Antioch, a large portion of whom were Gentiles, collected an offering for the Jerusalem church. In all of these responses of the Jewish believers, we see three important behaviors of inclusion:

1.   embracing,
2.   teaching, and
3.   receiving help.

These are truths we can apply in our own relationships within the body of Christ. We can fight *for* people rather than against them.

Daily Wrap-Up

What is one way you noticed God at work in Acts 11?

How did the believers respond?

Extra Insight

In Acts 11, we find the first mention of *elders* in the church at Jerusalem.[12]

Though we didn't see God sending fire or visions, we saw His Spirit open wide the doors for more people to hear about Christ. God helped Peter explain the changes in thought he had experienced so that others could understand the shift to Gentile inclusion. The people responded by listening and being willing to change long-held mindsets in order to welcome new believers into the church. Believers such as Barnabas rejoiced when they saw for themselves the Lord working among the Gentiles. Gentiles in turn collected money to help out their Jewish brothers and sisters in Christ. The more we know and understand God and His message, the more our lives overflow with His qualities such as generosity, compassion, and freedom.

Today we focused on this truth: *determining essentials helps us enjoy traditions rather than become enslaved by them.*

How would you summarize your personal takeaway from today's lesson?

I am grateful that God doesn't practice favoritism so that I am able to receive His grace. I want to pursue essentials and enjoy traditions, being able to distinguish between them so that I don't push my preferences on others. As we awaken more and more to God's power, message, and freedom, we want to camp on things that will matter in eternity rather than nitpick over small differences of opinion.

Talk with God

Lord, show me what to hold tightly and what to hold loosely. Awaken me to the freedom I have in You. Thank You that I am under grace, not law. Help me to walk in that grace and see You at work in my everyday life. Show me how to include others by extending Your invitation of peace through Christ. Amen.

Memory Verse Exercise

Read the Memory Verse on page 74 several times, and then fill in the blanks below as you recite it:

Then _____ replied, "I see _____ _____ that God shows no _____. In every nation he _____ those who _____ _____ and do what is right. This is the _____ of Good News for the people of _____ —that there is _____ with _____ through Jesus Christ, who is Lord of all."

(Acts 10:34-36)

Day 3: Freedom from Bondage

Big Idea

We can experience internal freedom through Christ even when we aren't released from binding circumstances.

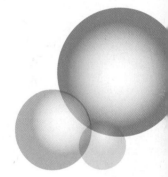

My friend anticipated the weeklong vacation where she would be released from the bondage of the daily grind. No alarm clocks. No schedule. Good friends. This was her recipe for freedom. However, the week turned out to be emotionally exhausting as conflicts arose within the friend group, resulting in gossip, factions, and unrest.

Have you ever looked forward to circumstances you thought would bring freedom only to experience difficulty instead? Write anything that comes to mind:

I've often believed freedom would come in the form of an empty calendar. But when unforeseen circumstances cleared my schedule, I found myself aimless, sleepless, and struggling more than I could have imagined. Sometimes we don't realize that we are holding on to the wrong freedom dream for ourselves until we're in the midst of it.

This same friend of mine whose vacation went awry recalled a time the opposite happened in her life. She was expecting bondage from a particular situation and found incredible freedom instead. Well, not bondage exactly. She planned to work at a summer camp for six weeks and dreaded the uncomfortable beds and demanding work schedule. While it was physically exhausting and uncomfortable, she can't remember a time she felt so connected to the Lord and others. Our ideas about what will bring us freedom are not always accurate.

In Acts 12, we will continue our theme of awakening to freedom. The Lord has opened Peter's eyes to freedom from favoritism and tradition, and now Peter and his friend James will both experience freedom in a very physical sense. However, it will play out very differently in their circumstances.

Read Acts 12:1-5 and describe the circumstances for each man:

James (the brother of John):

Peter:

Extra Insight

The James mentioned here was not the brother of Jesus who became a leader of the Jerusalem church and wrote the New Testament Book of James.

The shape of freedom here looks like death and bondage. However, if we believe the gospel, James's death ends in freedom as he meets Christ face to face. And Peter finds himself in literal bondage, shackles and all.

What does the church do when Peter ends up in chains for preaching the good news? (v. 5)

What situation in your life or the lives of those you love has caused you to pray very earnestly?

Throughout Acts we will continue to find awakening to God inextricably linked to prayer. Maybe the situation you wrote about led you to pray for protection, blessing, or direction. Sometimes our earnest prayers echo those of the early church, asking God for freedom. We may not need release from physical chains, but our emotional and mental bondage can be just as paralyzing. Pornography, food addiction, anger, and other entanglements threaten to keep us from fully awakening to God. Let's see what happened as the church prayed.

Read Acts 12:6-19, and choose one of these two options:

In the empty prison cell, complete the scene by drawing Peter, the chains, the soldiers, and the angel:

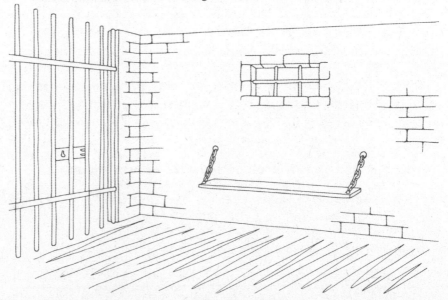

In three to four bullet points, tell what happened:

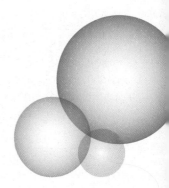

-

-

-

-

I love that Peter thought this jailbreak was a dream. Perhaps the memory of his rooftop vision caused him to think he might be hallucinating. Regardless, God supernaturally set him free in answer to the church's earnest prayers. Stories like this inspire me to pray, and they also cause me to question why sometimes we storm the throne of heaven with great fervor but the worst happens. Our family prayed for my uncle to be healed, but he died a painful death. I wonder if you ever have prayed earnestly and wondered why God didn't answer according to your definition of freedom. We know He can give us what we ask. After all, He sent an angel to free Peter. When studying passages like this one, we need to consider the whole of Scripture to bring balance.

Read Hebrews 11:33-38 and then answer the question below.

By faith these people overthrew kingdoms, ruled with justice, and received what God had promised them. They shut the mouths of lions, quenched the flames of fire, and escaped death by the edge of the sword. Their weakness was turned to strength. They became strong in battle and put whole armies to flight. Women received their loved ones back again from death.

But others were tortured, refusing to turn from God in order to be set free. They placed their hope in a better life after the Resurrection. Some were jeered at, and their backs were cut open with whips. Others were chained in prisons. Some died by stoning, some were sawed in half, and others were killed with the sword. Some went about wearing skins of sheep and goats, destitute and oppressed and mistreated. They were too good for this world, wandering over deserts and mountains, hiding in caves and holes in the ground.

All these people earned a good reputation because of their faith, yet none of them received all that God had promised. For God had something better in mind for us, so that they would not reach perfection without us.

The physical cause of Herod's symptoms might have been "appendicitis leading to peritonitis" with the addition of roundworms, which were common at that time due to poor "medical hygiene." Another scholar suggests that a cyst produced by a tapeworm could have been the cause.[14]

Based on these verses, what do we learn about the relationship between faithfulness and "circumstantial freedom"? In other words, does our faithfulness always lead to our literal freedom?

Sometimes God supernaturally steps in, and sometimes He doesn't. But either way, God is always at work. We can pray for what we think freedom from bondage looks like, but ultimately, we must surrender our wills to the Lord, trusting that His answer of freedom is best.

Christ's death on a cross initially did not seem like freedom to the disciples, but eventually they understood what Jesus's death and resurrection accomplished. There is a gap between our understanding of freedom and God's good plan for our freedom that requires trust. We will see this illustrated again in the last few verses of Acts 12.

King Herod seemed to have all the power, being free to kill and imprison people. But his freedom wasn't all that it seemed.

Read Acts 12:20-25, and record below how Herod's apparent freedom ended:

Herod accepted the worship of people, and he was consumed by worms and died. Freedom isn't always what it seems. What looks like freedom might actually be bondage to sin. Conversely, what looks like difficulties might bring inner freedom as we grow in peace, contentment, and joy in the midst of our trials. Whether your circumstances are challenging or fairly easy, I pray you are experiencing God's freedom in your spirit as you navigate the highs and lows in your life.

Daily Wrap-Up

What is one way you noticed God at work in Acts 12?

How did the believers respond?

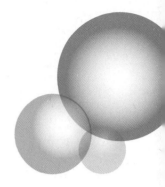

God sent angels to display His power in setting Peter free and worms to consume King Herod as a result of his refusal to give praise to God. The people of God spread the message about Jesus and prayed earnestly.

Today we focused on this truth: *we can experience internal freedom through Christ even when we aren't released from binding circumstances.*

How would you summarize your personal takeaway from today's lesson?

We might see more divine intervention in our lives as we awaken to God's freedom as the early believers did, or perhaps we will have to trust God more in the absence of miraculous intervention. Either way, we can experience inner freedom as we overcome whatever bondage we are fighting.

Talk with God

Lord, free me from bondage. I don't have to live entangled by sin because You died to set me free. Help me to cultivate peace, contentment, and joy even in the midst of my current difficulties. I also ask for freedom from bondage for all those literally imprisoned because of their faith in You. I earnestly pray for You to release them in Jesus's name, just as You released Peter! I know You are able. Amen.

Memory Verse Exercise

Read the Memory Verse on page 74 several times, and then fill in the blanks below as you recite it:

*Then _____ replied, "I see _____ _____ that
God _____ no _____. In every nation he
_____ those who _____ _____ and do what is right.
This is the _____ of Good _____ for the people of
_____—that there is _____ with _____ through Jesus
_____, who is Lord of _____."*

(Acts 10:34-36)

Big Idea

Once we experience freedom in Christ, we want to share it with others.

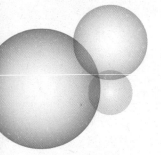

Extra Insight

Saul's Jewish name has been used up to this point, but in Acts 13 Luke transitions to his Roman name, Paul. This occurs alongside the shift from Jewish to Gentile audiences.[15]

Day 4: Freedom to Share

I asked women on social media to share their stories of freedom from destructive patterns. These were the first two responses:

"I was a former compara-holic who later realized my breast implants were now making me sick. Having them removed resulted in freedom from the health complications I had suffered. I share my story so other women are able to authentically see what comparing ourselves can do—and the freedom that we have when we live how God created us to be."

"I remember when 'someone' hurt my family. I held this 'someone' captive in my thoughts and heart for a long time. She never knew about how I allowed her to steal my joy. I realized many months later that I needed to surrender that hurt and 'someone' to the Lord and let Christ give me freedom and forgiveness."

Whether or not you can relate to these examples, how have you been able to encourage others who have walked through challenges similar to those you have experienced?

When we find freedom, it gives us joy to share it with others. As women responded to my question on social media, they shared about the freedom they have found from things such as:

- hating their sexual abuser,
- letting their inability to say no rule their lives,
- pleasing people,
- being driven by their emotions, or
- allowing alcoholism to control their lives.

Whether you've struggled with these or other issues, once you've taken a spiritual breath of sweet freedom, you want to look for ways to help others. All of us once lived in bondage to sin, but as believers in Christ, we have freedom to live according to the Holy Spirit instead of our sinful natures. Saul knew personally how living by the law contrasted with freedom in Christ. He zealously followed his Pharisee training and persecuted followers of Jesus whose message of grace threatened his deep-rooted belief in law. His life changed radically when he encountered Christ on the road to Damascus. After his radical transformation, Saul:

- stayed with believers in Damascus for a few days and began preaching immediately (Acts 9:19-20),
- preached with the apostles in Jerusalem and debated the Jews (Acts 9:28-29),
- went to Caesarea where he was sent to his hometown of Tarsus (Acts 9:30), and
- was found in Tarsus by Barnabas and brought to Antioch where he taught large crowds for a year (Acts 11:25-26).

In the years following his conversion, he shared the freedom he had found through living by the Holy Spirit rather than by a set of rules.

Read Acts 13:1-3 and note below what activities the early church leaders (including Saul) practiced at the time the Holy Spirit gave them clear directions:

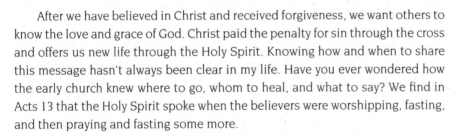

After we have believed in Christ and received forgiveness, we want others to know the love and grace of God. Christ paid the penalty for sin through the cross and offers us new life through the Holy Spirit. Knowing how and when to share this message hasn't always been clear in my life. Have you ever wondered how the early church knew where to go, whom to heal, and what to say? We find in Acts 13 that the Holy Spirit spoke when the believers were worshipping, fasting, and then praying and fasting some more.

What connection might we make between their spiritual activities and their ability to hear the Holy Spirit speaking?

God spoke through a donkey (Numbers 22:28), through an angel striking Peter to wake him (Acts 12:7), and through a light that blinded Saul on the road to Damascus (Acts 9). The Holy Spirit isn't limited in when and how He speaks, and He actually lives within those of us who follow Christ. God is always communicating, and we *can* hear Him more clearly when we practice listening.

Are there spiritual activities or practices that help you to hear from the Lord? If so, write about them below:

So far in our study of Acts, we've seen the Holy Spirit's presence associated with believers engaging in these types of things:

- meeting together (Acts 2:1-4; 11:28);
- repenting of sin, turning to God, being baptized (Acts 2:38; 8:16);
- preaching (Acts 4:8; 11:15);
- praying (Acts 4:31; 8:15);
- being obedient (Acts 5:32);
- sharing their faith (Acts 8:29-39);
- living in fear of the Lord (Acts 9:31);
- reflecting (Acts 10:19);
- listening (Acts 10:44); and
- worshipping and fasting (Acts 13:2).

Extra Insight

The name Bar-Jesus means "son of Jesus," which provides a play on words for Paul's declaration of him as a "son of the devil" in Acts 13:10.[16]

Put a star by any of the above activities you sense the Lord calling you to pursue more intentionally.

The Lord invites us to ask for wisdom (James 1:5), and I believe He wants to give us clear guidance in how to share our story of freedom in Christ. Acts 13 marks a significant shift in Acts as we witness Saul's first of three missionary journeys. So many rich truths are packed into these verses, but we will focus on how the Holy Spirit guided people like Saul to share the good news about Jesus.

Read Acts 13:4-12 and note the two mentions of the Holy Spirit. Write below the verbs associated with the Spirit's work:

Verse 4:

Verse 9:

The first stop on the journey was Cyprus, Barnabas's hometown (Acts 4:36). The Spirit sent and filled Paul while in Cyprus, enabling him to boldly rebuke deception so that the proconsul, or governor, could find freedom in Christ. The same Spirit that lived in Paul and Barnabas lives in us. Prayer is one of the ways the Holy Spirit guides us.

Choose one or both of the following prayer prompts, and write a personal prayer below it.

For direction to know where God is calling me to spread His message:

For boldness to share my beliefs even when others oppose them:

As a consummate conflict-avoider, I don't like to disagree with people. I'm asking for boldness to lovingly share my faith even when others mock or oppose it.

Paul and Barnabas continued to travel as the Spirit led them to share the message with different audiences. After leaving Cyprus, they set out by ship for Pamphylia. John Mark left them, but Paul and Barnabas traveled inland to Antioch of Pisidia. In the synagogue, Paul was invited to share words of encouragement.

If you have the time, read Acts 13:13-37, but if you need the CliffsNotes version, here is a summary of what Paul preached in these verses:

- God chose our ancestors and led them out of slavery in Egypt where they wandered in the wilderness for forty years and then conquered the land of Canaan, settling there.
- In Canaan, judges ruled until God gave Israel a king named Saul, who later was replaced by David.
- David was a man after God's heart, and his descendant Jesus is God's promised Savior.
- John the Baptist preached about Jesus coming, but the leaders and people in Jerusalem eventually rejected and killed Jesus.
- God raised Jesus from the dead, and He appeared to many witnesses.
- Psalm 16:10 testifies of Jesus as the Son of God who would not rot in a grave.

All this background information has been building toward a climax.

Read Acts 13:38-43. How did Paul describe freedom in Christ? (vv. 38-39)

Extra Insight

The place referred to as Antioch Pisidia is not the same Antioch where Saul and Barnabas started their journey and spent a year teaching. Several cities were founded by a man who named them all after his father, Antiochus.[17]

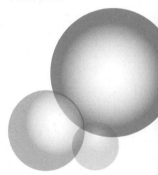

What did Paul and Barnabas urge the new believers to continue to rely on? (v. 43)

Our freedom story is the one Paul described. We have forgiveness of sins and are declared right with God not because of our rule-following, good works, or human effort but by the grace of God alone. I need to be regularly reminded not to fall back into works mode.

Are you fully relying on the grace of God right now? If not, where in your life do you need to rely on the grace of God rather than your own efforts?

The difference between trying and trusting gets blurred for me on a regular basis. When my spiritual life feels like a chore list to be checked off, I know I need to get back to grace. To all who would listen, Paul kept teaching and preaching to walk in God's freedom and live by the Spirit rather than the flesh. I've found that when I experience freedom, it usually is tested right away.

Read Acts 13:44-52 and answer the following questions:

Who opposed Paul and why? (v. 45)

To whom did Paul and Barnabas say they would offer the message now? (v. 46)

How did the Gentiles respond? (v. 48)

With what two things were the believers filled? (v. 52)

Previously we've seen that Philip shared the gospel with an Ethiopian and Peter saw Cornelius's household saved, yet Acts 13 marks a shift in the gospel movement. Now the Gentiles not only will be *included* when God supernaturally intervenes, they also will be intentionally *pursued* with the gospel message. This concept may seem normal to us, but it wasn't for the original audience of Luke's account. Christianity had been considered a minority group within Judaism. The pivot in Acts 13 will grow Christianity's reputation to a majority religion over time.

Throughout the spread of the gospel, Christ followers endured much hardship, but they also were filled with joy. Joy isn't the same as happiness. Joy is from the Greek word *chara*,[18] which comes from the word *charis*,[19] which means grace. Real joy denotes a gladness not dependent on circumstances but on the grace of God. We can't manufacture it, but we can receive it.

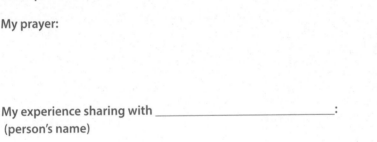

How has sharing your story of freedom in Christ with others brought you joy? If you aren't sure how to answer, ask the Holy Spirit to lead you this week to one person with whom you can share your story of awakening to freedom. Write a short prayer in the space below. Then come back later and add the person's name and a brief description of the experience.

My prayer:

My experience sharing with _____:
(person's name)

Jesus died to buy our freedom. He wants to apply that freedom to every part of our lives. We can't be free in our own strength, but change is possible through the Holy Spirit.

Daily Wrap-Up

What is one way you noticed God at work in Acts 13?

How did the believers respond?

The Holy Spirit commissioned, sent, and filled Paul so that he could be God's instrument. His life wasn't easy, but he found joy sharing the good news about forgiveness and grace with others. Some responded to this message with belief, and others opposed and persecuted the messengers.

Today we focused on this truth: *once we experience freedom in Christ, we want to share it with others.*

How would you summarize your personal takeaway from today's lesson?

Our missionary journeys may not take us to islands but to grocery stores and community meetings. In our own strength, we feel tongue-tied and scared, but with God's Spirit we find freedom to share our stories. Our responsibility is not to force spiritual freedom on anyone but, instead, to share the message that has the power to awaken people to God in everyday life.

Talk with God

Lord, help me to stop striving to live for You in my own strength. Show me what it looks like to listen and obey the leading of Your Spirit. Awaken me to worship, prayer, and fasting so that I may receive direction and filling from You. Show me how I can share Your message of freedom and experience greater joy as I serve You on my own missionary journeys. Amen.

Memory Verse Exercise

Read the Memory Verse on page 74 several times, and then fill in the blanks below as you recite it:

Then _____ _____, "I see _____ _____
that God _____ no _____. In _____
nation he _____ _____ who _____ _____ and do
what is _____. This is the _____ of Good _____
for the _____ of _____—that _____
is _____ with _____ through _____ _____,
who is Lord of _____."

(Acts 10:34-36)

Day 5: Freedom to Focus

This morning I opened my laptop without a clear plan of which task I would tackle first. I needed to listen to an online teaching at some point in the day, so I went to the website and started the video. After a few minutes, I brought up another tab because I realized I needed to cancel a subscription before I got charged for something I don't use anymore. Then I decided to scoot over to my email and just take a peek. Before I knew it, I was lost in answering, deleting, and filing emails. All of a sudden, the video stopped, and I realized I hadn't heard a word in quite some time and needed to start over. Can you relate?

What struggles have you encountered recently related to your ability to focus?

Big Idea

When we awaken to God's freedom, we find the power to change our focus.

I've heard many allusions to women being able to multitask. According to a study done at the Cleveland Clinic, "When we think we're multitasking, most often we aren't really doing two things at once, but instead, we're doing individual actions in rapid succession."[20] The neuroscience is clear: we are wired to be mono-taskers. What we learn from science proves true in our own routines: our focus can be on only one thing at a time.

Awakening to God in everyday life frees us to focus on God amid all the distractions that vie for our attention. I can put the things that distract me from God in a few categories:

- **Focus on self:** I'm hyper-aware of my desire for pleasure and comfort. I like food that delights me, shows that entertain me, health that doesn't limit me, people who look out for me, and the money to finance all of those things. Did you notice how many times the word *me* appears in the previous sentence?
- **Focus on what others think:** Applause makes me feel good, and criticism dampens my mood quickly. It can be a roller-coaster ride full of ups and downs that provides insecurity rather than a thrill.
- **Focus on struggles or pain:** Life is hard. Cancer, divorce, difficulties in ministry, relational conflict, and so many other real problems swirl around in my head.
- **Focus on busyness:** Working, cooking, cleaning, discipling, parenting, and all the things that fill my calendar can take center stage in my life

Extra Insight

Several of the cities in Paul's first missionary journey were the hometowns of notable disciples. Barnabas grew up on the island of Cyprus while Paul's mentee, Timothy, was from Lystra. Another man we'll meet in Acts 20, named Gaius, was from Derbe.[21]

so that I'm rushing all the time. Then when I have a free moment, I want to escape with food or entertainment.

Of these categories of distractions, which one most strikes a chord with you today? If none of them does, feel free to name another category of distractions:

Extra Insight

The Romans subdivided Galatia into regions including Isauria, Pisidia, Phrygia, and Lycaonia. The letter Paul sent the Galatians would have been read by churches spread throughout these regions.[22]

Don't hear me say that taking care of your health or enjoying leisure time is sinful. Self-care and soul care are important practices. Also, God created work, so it's not wrong to have a to-do list. We just have to be careful not to make these things the predominant focus of our lives. They can be practices in our relationship with and worship of God, or they can become distractions that lead us away from Him. As we talk about focus today, we will discover the freedom we have to keep our attention on God in spite of the influence of our sinful nature, the reactions of those around us, suffering, and overflowing to-do lists.

As we read Acts 14, we will look for the focus of the early church and consider where we might need to wake up. We can ask ourselves whether our focus falls more in line with our current culture or the disciples of Christ. Satan loves to keep us stuck in patterns, believing we will always be focused on temporal things such as food, stuff, comfort, or others' opinions. When we awaken to God's freedom, we find the power to change our focus.

The Holy Spirit can transform us so that whether people throw roses or stones our way, we are not deterred in our pursuit of God. That's exactly what happened to Paul and Barnabas on the last leg of their first missionary journey. Let's take a brief look at where they have traveled so far.

Let's look at a map of Paul's first missionary journey so we can envision the route he traveled with Barnabas. This map gives us an idea of how far Paul and Barnabas have come, where they are right now, and where they are headed next.

On the map on page 99, trace Paul and Barnabas's route using your finger or pen, starting at Seleucia and stopping at Antioch in the region of Pisidia (end of arrow segment 4). Circle the city of Antioch.

Antioch in Pisidia is where we left the disciples in our study yesterday. Today we will see them cover a lot of ground in twenty-eight short verses.

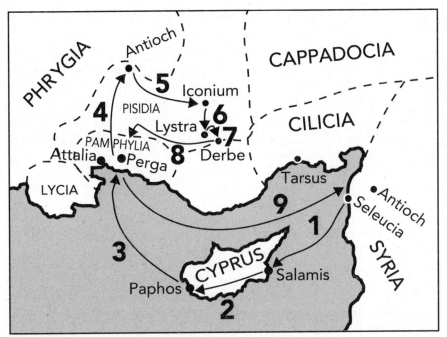

Read Acts 14:1-7 and record the information noted below:

The name of the city (v. 1):

The focus of their message (v. 3):

Different responses to their message (vv. 1, 2, 4, 5):

Paul and Barnabas preached boldly about the grace of God. Some believed, and others threw stones—as in they hurled big rocks at them!

As you reflect on your Christian journey, how have those around you responded differently to your faith?

Many of my family members and friends follow Jesus, but even within the church and Christian friendships, I've encountered sharp opposition to what I sensed was God's leading in my life. I've also had neighbors who didn't understand my radical belief in Jesus. They may have laughed at my expense a few times, but they never *threw* anything at me.

Extra Insights

"Stoning was normally intended to be fatal."[24]

In his Letter to the Galatians, Paul might have been referring to the marks left from his stoning in Lystra when he wrote, "From now on, don't let anyone trouble me with these things. For I bear on my body the scars that show I belong to Jesus" (Galatians 6:17).

Too many times I have gauged my faithfulness by the responses of others around me. Paul and Barnabas seemed to anticipate a fickle crowd. From my perspective as a modern reader of the text, I wonder why the people of Iconium would want to stone travelers who healed their sick and performed supernatural wonders. I appreciate the insight of scholar Craig Keener when it comes to making sense of signs throughout the Book of Acts. He said, "Signs do not guarantee belief; they merely make the message impossible to ignore, usually demanding faith or rejection. Yet they appear important for the gospel breaking into new regions (Romans 15:18-19; 2 Corinthians 12:12)."[23]

The abundance of miracles in Paul's missionary journeys drew attention to the good news in places where it never had been heard. We find another one of these signs in Acts 14.

Read verses 8-20 and fill in the blanks in the storyboard using the word bank below. (If you have trouble, use the New Living Translation.)

Word Bank: Jews, Zeus, healed, human, walking, die, feet, Hermes

1.	2.	3.	4.	5.	6.	7.
Paul and Barnabas come upon a man with crippled _____ (v. 8)	Paul looked at him and realized he had the faith to be _____ (v. 9)	The man jumped to his feet and started _____ (v. 10)	The people decided Paul and Barnabas were the gods _____ and _____ and began to worship them (v. 12)	Paul and Barnabas told them they were _____ like them and explained the gospel to them using nature as a starting point (v. 15)	Some _____ from Antioch and Iconium turned the crowd against them and stoned Paul (v. 19)	Paul didn't _____, and he and Barnabas left for Derbe the next day (vv. 19-20)

At first the people worshipped Paul and Barnabas, thinking them to be Zeus and Hermes. The local villagers were familiar with a tale in which Zeus and Hermes visited their city disguised as mortals. According to the legend, only one family welcomed them. That family was rewarded by Zeus and Hermes with their straw hut being transformed with a gold roof and marble columns. However, the inhospitable had their homes destroyed.[25] The people of Lystra didn't want to make the same mistake as their ancestors in the fable, so they worshipped Paul and Barnabas, supposing that they were indeed Zeus and Hermes returning to their land. This information helps us understand this reaction of a mystical peasant population who spoke their own dialect and did not have access to Greek or Roman philosophy and education.[26]

While no one has gathered garlands and sacrificed oxen to worship you, have you ever experienced a time when people overly recognized or elevated you? If not, can you think of any people you might overly idealize?

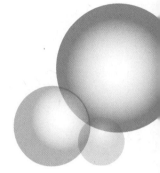

We humans have a tendency to idolize other people. The Galatians were just more overt in their methods than we are generally. Maybe we read everything someone posts online and quote them all the time. Even within Christianity we can put communicators, worship leaders, pastors, and authors on a pedestal that beckons a fall. We can learn to appreciate those who utilize their God-given gifts without focusing on the messenger more than the message. God has given us freedom so that we can focus on Him rather than on His instruments.

Paul focused not only on the message but also on his audience. As an educated debater, Paul didn't use Scripture or philosophy as we later will see Him utilize in Samaria and Athens. In this region, Paul pointed to nature, something an agrarian society would have appreciated and connected with deity. He talked about rain, food, and good crops to point to God (v. 17).

As we focus on God and the people He has put in our lives, we can use our freedoms of time and energy to share the good news about Christ in a way that our audience can best receive it.

Think of one person you are praying would believe in Christ. Write his or her name below:

Name: _____

Now, in the margin, write a prayer for this person to know Christ:

God awakens us to freedom, but it's freedom to focus on Him rather than on people-pleasing, stuff, or self. As we focus on Him, we want others to know His freedom. We also want to encourage and help other believers.

Read Acts 14:21-28 and record below and on the following page at least three things that Paul and Barnabas did for the Christians on their journey back through the towns in which they had preached (Lystra, Iconium, and Antioch of Pisidia):

(v. 22)

(v. 23)

(v. 25)

Paul and Barnabas strengthened, encouraged, and reminded the new Christians about suffering. I can't remember the last time a leader, mentor, or friend reminded me about the suffering associated with following Christ and living on this broken planet. Even if you hear that message more often than I do, so much of the American Dream with its pursuit of happiness has seeped into our Western gospel that we are prone to forget that God didn't promise us a life of ease. But He did promise His presence, peace, and power.

Paul knew firsthand about suffering, yet when left for dead, he got up and kept doing the things that had landed him in a pile of stones. His focus on God evidenced itself in how he persevered through trials with a greater goal in mind.

I want to wake up to that same mission so that my sufferings do not easily derail me. At the end of the first missionary journey, we find the church engaging again in prayer and fasting.

As you consider what captures your focus lately, what is one practical way you can turn your focus toward God today?

Prayer is a key practice that helps us focus on God. Fasting takes away the distraction of food (or whatever we are fasting from) for even greater concentration. I'm asking the Lord for help so that I turn my focus from idolizing people and my own comfort to fully awakening to God—in the little things as well as the big. I want God to be the center of how I spend my time, money, and thoughts. As we near the halfway point of Acts, I pray that awakening to God in everyday life is shifting your focus as well!

Daily Wrap-Up

What is one way you noticed God at work in Acts 14?

How did the believers respond?

We saw that the Lord enabled Paul and Barnabas to preach with power so that both Jews and Greeks became believers. We also saw the Lord use Paul and Barnabas to heal a crippled man. Stones that should have killed Paul didn't stop the ministry the Lord wanted to do through him. Paul and Barnabas responded by continuing to teach, encourage, and strengthen the believers in faith. They didn't focus on their sufferings but on sharing the gospel message so that more people could find freedom in knowing Christ.

Today we focused on this truth: *when we awaken to God's freedom, we find the power to change our focus.*

How would you summarize your personal takeaway from today's lesson?

We may or may not see signs and wonders, but we can ask for eyes to see how God softens hearts, answers prayer, and invites every person into relationship with Him. Often, we discover this in quiet reflection and daily habits that help us to focus on the Lord. When we take time to listen, we can respond to those around us with grace, truth, and love. Whether we're in church or at the store, looking at a screen or walking in nature, alone or with people, we can awaken to the freedom to focus on the Lord. When our eyes are fixed on His kingdom, the distractions of this life lose their power to steal our gaze.

Talk with God

Lord, help me to focus on You. I easily get consumed with watching other people's lives, my own thoughts, and the suffering all around me. I want to bring all of these things to You instead of overthinking them. Free me to focus on Your good news and share it with others. Wake me up to believe that Your mission is worth the suffering and sacrifice. Thank You for being present and powerful even in the midst of the difficulties of following You. In Jesus's name. Amen.

Memory Verse Exercise

Read the Memory Verse on page 74 several times, and then fill in the blanks below as you recite it:

_____ _____ _____, "I see _____
_____ that _____ _____ no _____.
In _____ _____ he _____ _____ who
_____ _____ and do _____ is _____. _____ is the
_____ of _____ _____ for the _____ of
_____—that _____ is _____ with _____ through
_____ _____, who is _____ of _____."

(Acts 10:34-36)

Weekly Wrap-Up

Review the Big Idea for each day, and then write any personal application that comes to mind.

Day 1: Freedom from Favoritism

Big Idea: as we awaken to see people the way God does, we can cross the boundaries of difference and find freedom from favoritism.

Personal Application:_____

_____

Day 2: Freedom from Tradition

Big Idea: determining essentials helps us enjoy traditions rather than become enslaved by them.

Personal Application:_____

_____

Day 3: Freedom from Bondage

Big Idea: we can experience internal freedom through Christ even when we aren't released from binding circumstances.

Personal Application:_____

_____

Day 4: Freedom to Share

Big Idea: once we experience freedom in Christ, we want to share it with others.

Personal Application:_____

_____

Day 5: Freedom to Focus

Big Idea: when we awaken to God's freedom, we find the power to change our focus.

Personal Application:_____

_____

Video Viewer Guide: Week 3

Legalism is "strict adherence to _____ or prescription, especially to the _____ rather than the _____."

We have to find our identity in the person of _____ rather than the patterns of _____.

Acts 10:34-36; 44-45

We must release _____ _____ in order to embrace _____.

Freedom is not getting what we _____ but what we _____.

Galatians 5:1

Expect some _____ _____ when you take _____ _____.

Acts 11:1-3

Acts 11:15-18

Action step: What is one step you can take toward greater freedom?

Week 4

Awakening to God's Grace

Acts 15–19

Memory Verse

"We believe that we are all saved the same way, by the undeserved grace of the Lord Jesus."

(Acts 15:11)

Day 1: Grace to Disagree

My friend says, "There is no pain like church pain." Often church pain cuts deeply because it originates from unexpected sources. The people I prayed and studied the Bible alongside weren't the ones I expected to gossip and harshly judge me. But I have met and talked with so many women who have had similar experiences.

I am in an online Facebook group created for women in ministry who need a safe place to share their struggles, and I have read story after story of disagreement and discouragement. No one has to convince us that the church isn't immune to disagreement and conflict. We've either experienced it personally or watched it from afar.

What sorts of disagreements have you encountered whether they've been within church, family, friendship, work, or other settings?

Big Idea

Because believers don't agree on everything, we need God's grace to work through our varying viewpoints.

I know a woman who said her women's ministry committee didn't hold their annual retreat because the discussion over whether to serve salads or subs got too heated. I've seen believers misunderstand one another's social media posts. Some have disagreed over theology, methodology, or leadership roles. None of this, however, is new. From its infancy, the church needed God's grace to sort through both corporate and personal disagreements.

As we awaken to God's grace in our lives, we learn to extend that grace to others when we sort through disagreements, just as the church did in Acts. We'll find two different scenarios in today's reading. One was a churchwide disagreement over requirements for new believers, and another was a personal disagreement over a person.

When we left Paul and Barnabas last week, they had just returned from their first missionary journey.

Read Acts 15:1-21 and fill in the missing info below:

1. The men from Judea taught that you cannot be saved unless you are _____. (v. 1)

2. Paul and Barnabas reacted by _____. (v. 2)

3. The church decided to send_____ to

   _____. (vv. 3-4)

4. The apostles and elders _____. (v. 6)

5. _____ stood up and addressed the leaders after a long discussion. (v. 7)

6. He said, that we are all saved through _____. (v. 11)

7. After hearing from Peter and personal testimonies from Paul and Barnabas, _____ spoke up. (v. 13)

8. James made the judgment that _____. (v. 19)

Let's take a moment to review the major players:

Paul and Barnabas—They had just completed a missionary journey where they preached in Cyprus and the region of Galatia where they saw many Gentiles saved.

Peter—He is the Pentecost preacher who spoke boldly and later had a vision of food coming down on a sheet. This convinced him that the Gentiles could be saved.

James—He was the brother of Jesus who didn't believe in Him as the Messiah until after the Resurrection (Matthew 13:15; Galatians 1:19). He became the chief leader in the Jerusalem church[2] and author of the New Testament Book of James.

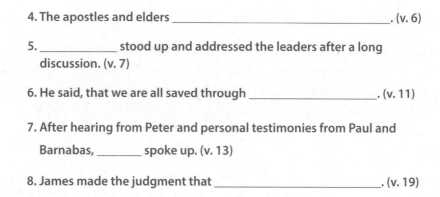

What was the main issue that divided the church in this passage?

By requiring circumcision for Gentile converts, the church would essentially be saying that a Gentile must become a Jew in order to be a Christian. Circumcision was the requirement for foreigners who wanted to convert to Judaism (Genesis 17:12-13; Exodus 12:48).

When you think about how the early church settled their disagreement, what stands out to you?

The church held a long discussion and included a plurality of leadership. One person didn't dominate or control the conversation. The early believers also took into consideration past history, present ramifications, and applications for the church going forward:

Answers: 1. circumcised; 2. arguing vehemently; 3. delegates, Jerusalem; 4. met to resolve the issue; 5. Peter; 6. Grace; 7. James; 8. they should not make it difficult for the Gentiles.

Past: Peter spoke about the vision of food and Cornelius's salvation that had occurred a decade earlier.[4]

Present: Paul and Barnabas gave testimonies of what they had seen God doing among the Gentiles on their recent missionary journey.

Future: James looked to the Scriptures and quoted from Amos 9:11-12, which was a reference to the future kingdom when Jesus returns. He helped the church apply grace to future theology and practical protocols with a decision not to make it difficult for Gentile believers.[5]

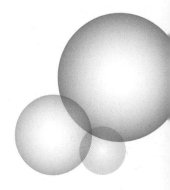

We see that the early church prioritized working out disagreements. They didn't keep arguing, resort to name calling, or start a new, separate group. Instead, they:

- traveled so they could talk face-to-face;
- discussed the matter at length;
- listened to one another, including several different leaders;
- considered what God had done in the past, how He was working in the present, and made connections with Scripture in regard to decisions; and
- seasoned their decision with grace.

If you are currently in a disagreement, how could you apply one of the early church's methods in your situation? (If you aren't, what principle might you keep in mind as something to remember for any future disagreements that might surface?)

Extra Insight

"A majority of scholars...identify the events of Gal 2:1-10 with Acts 15."[6] Paul's Letter to the Galatian churches (which he and Barnabas planted on their first missionary journey) describe this same Jerusalem council decision from Paul's perspective rather than Luke's.

Once the leaders made their decision, they put it in writing.

Read Acts 15:22-35 and check all the answers that apply.

What rules did the leaders ask the believers to abstain from? (v. 29)

❑ **Wearing shoes in the church building.**

❑ **Eating food offered to idols.**

❑ **Consuming blood or the meat of strangled animals.**

❑ **Arriving late to church meetings.**

❑ **Sexual immorality.**

What was the response of the people? (v. 31)

❏ Grumbling about rules.

❏ Insults aimed at church leaders.

❏ Great joy as they read the encouraging message.

What practices were displayed by believers? (vv. 32-35)

❏ Encouraging and strengthening their faith.

❏ Engaging in gossip regarding the unfairness of the instructions.

❏ Sending them on a journey with a blessing.

❏ Preaching the Word of the Lord.

❏ Leaving the church to find another with fewer rules.

The believers experienced joy and found encouragement in the decision. They strengthened one another and exchanged a blessing of peace. When the believers listened to one another, searched the Scriptures, and applied grace to the situation, they found joy in coming together in unity.

I can think of times in my marriage or friendships where conflict has strengthened relationships.

Can you think of an instance where you found peace, joy, and maybe even greater strength after working out a disagreement? If so, write about it below:

Sometimes we work out a conflict and come out stronger on the other side. Other times we can't force reconciliation and must walk away from a relationship in order to hold on to our convictions.

Read Acts 15:36-41 and summarize what happened between Paul and Barnabas:

John Mark was Barnabas's cousin. I know I have a soft spot where my family is concerned. Paul disagreed with Barnabas sharply. Until this point in Acts, Paul and Barnabas ministered together. They traveled, preached, healed, and encouraged. In fact, Barnabas's name means "son of encouragement."[7]

Yet when it came to including John Mark, Paul and Barnabas couldn't reach consensus, so Barnabas took John Mark, and Paul recruited a new partner named Silas. Both teams went on to fruitful ministry.

Accepting that disagreement leads to distance in a relationship can be difficult. I have personally experienced this when I tried to force reconciliation with friends and ministry partners. Yet the more we tried to come together, the more frustrated we got with each other. Being almost a decade on the other side of one such conflict, I can see how the Lord used both parties on separate paths, even when the rift was never fully mended. My peacemaker personality wanted everything tied with a neat bow, like the first account in Acts 15 where everyone comes together stronger. However, at times in our lives, God graciously allows us to separate and manages to multiply ministry in the process. He often takes our difficulties and uses them for good in our lives and for the benefit of others.

If you have ever seen a disagreement lead to a severed relationship, how can you look back on the situation and see the grace of God in it?

"Only Luke is with me. Bring Mark with you when you come, for he will be helpful to me in my ministry."
(2 Timothy 4:11)

"Aristarchus, who is in prison with me, sends you his greetings, and so does Mark, Barnabas's cousin. As you were instructed before, make Mark welcome if he comes your way."
(Colossians 4:10)

I love that many years after Luke wrote Acts, we get glimpses of grace in Paul and Barnabas's relationship.

We don't get many details, but what can you infer from the verses in the margin taken from Paul's letters written to Timothy and the church at Colossae? (Mark in these verses refers to John Mark in Acts 15.)

Extra Insight

Paul spoke favorably of John Mark in later years but also referenced Barnabas favorably in letters he wrote to the churches in Corinth, Galatia, and Colossae (1 Corinthians 9:6; Galatians 2:9; Colossians 4:10).

It seems that time and grace healed the fracture between Paul and Barnabas since Paul's love for John Mark evidenced itself in his letters. When we can't agree, we must accept God's grace in either a reconciliation or a separation.

Daily Wrap-Up

What is one way you noticed God at work in Acts 15?

How did God's people respond?

While we didn't see a display of divine intervention with angels, visions, or healings, we saw the Lord supernaturally help the church work through disagreements. His grace in helping us work toward unity takes no less a miracle than releasing prison shackles. Relationships are hard. We awaken to God's grace as we respond to God by listening and learning in our conflicts.

Today we focused on this truth: *because believers don't agree on everything, we need God's grace to work through our varying viewpoints.*

How would you summarize your personal takeaway from today's lesson?

Conflicts often bring strong emotions to the surface. Anger, fear, and sadness in conflicts can skew our ability to see things clearly. We can press into God's grace and allow Him to heal and help so that we can allow His grace to spill over in our relationships. Because of His love and stability, we find hope and accept His leading, whether a relationship grows closer or further apart.

Talk with God

Lord, I don't like conflict. Sometimes I wonder why believers can't be more aligned. Help us to find unity and act lovingly—especially when we disagree. Lord, give me the strength to listen and learn from others who hold different views. Help me to grow through struggle and trust You for the outcome. Awaken me to Your grace so that I can extend it to others! Amen.

Memory Verse Exercise

Read the Memory Verse on page 106 several times, and then fill in the blanks below as you recite it:

We _____ that we are all saved the same way, by the undeserved _____ of the Lord Jesus.

(Acts 15:11)

Day 2: Grace to Show Deference

More than twenty years ago, my husband joined the staff at a church where we had years of relational connection with the senior pastor and his wife. We were less familiar with the church where they served but knew we agreed with their doctrinal statement. Many denominations have preferences about their mode of baptism or Communion, and this particular church practiced baptism by immersing believers three times with a forward motion. My husband and I had previously been baptized, but not in this exact way.

No one required re-baptism, but my husband knew that some older members were staunch in their adherence to this particular mode. He decided to get baptized to show deference to those who might struggle with the young, new youth pastor coming from a different church background, and he invited me to join him. I initially felt that choosing to be baptized again would undermine the authenticity of my original baptism. It was an example from Acts 16 that helped me decide to join my husband in an act of deference. I yielded to an unnecessary practice to remove any barriers in necessary relationships.

Have you ever made a decision in order to defer for the sake of relationship? (If so, write the decision below.)

Big Idea

Awakening to God's grace results in valuing relationships over rules.

We need to take caution, however, in making decisions just to please people. There is a distinct difference between simply trying to please people and showing deference to them or their beliefs. The churches in Galatia (that are part of this second missionary journey in Acts 16) received a letter from Paul that said, "If pleasing people were my goal, I would not be Christ's servant" (Galatians 1:10b). Yet in this lesson, we find Paul removing stumbling blocks that might cause people to trip spiritually.

This week we focus on awakening to God's grace, but I struggled with the right word that would describe the postures we find in Acts 16. Words like *yield*, *humility*, *grace*, and *deference* came to mind as I read the chapter. *Deference* can feel like a dated word, but perhaps it is one that grace-filled believers need to bring back into use. If you aren't familiar with it, I hope that today's lesson will be filled with discovery rather than frustration in exploring this term that might feel unfamiliar. The dictionary defines *deference* as "humble submission and respect."[8] It doesn't mean people-pleasing or letting people treat you like a doormat, but in today's chapter, we'll find that:

- deference does unnecessary things to preserve necessary relationships,
- deference allows the Holy Spirit to guide our decisions,
- deference recognizes that God opens the hearts of people to His message,

"The Spirit is called here uniquely *the Spirit of Jesus*, a phrase which emphasizes how Jesus himself through the Spirit was guiding the progress of the gospel."[10]

"*Philippi* was an ancient town which had been renamed by Philip of Macedon in 360 BC. It was the site of the defeat of Julius Caesar's murderers, Brutus and Cassius, by Antony and Octavian…in 42 BC." During the writing of Acts, it was a Roman colony where many soldiers settled.[11]

- deference is willing to prolong physical oppression for another's spiritual freedom, and
- deference doesn't mean we cower at injustice.

As we tackle the first principle of deference, we need to remember that in Acts 15, the Jerusalem council decided that circumcision was not required for Gentile believers.

Read Acts 16:1-5 and briefly describe who Paul met and what he did to him:

Deference does unnecessary things to preserve necessary relationships.

Paul's circumcision of Timothy can seem counterintuitive to the decision Paul just argued. I wonder why Paul would do to Timothy what he preached was unnecessary for others. Verse 4 tells us they went from town to town instructing the believers to follow the decisions made by the Jerusalem council.

We learn from this example that sometimes believers do unnecessary things to preserve necessary relationships. Paul valued relationships over rules and removed any barriers he could foresee that would detract from the gospel message. Paul continued to practice deference, not just to people but to God's Holy Spirit.

Deference allows the Holy Spirit to guide our decisions.

Read Acts 16:6-10 and summarize Paul's vision in a sentence:

Paul didn't lay out an itinerary and ask God to bless his plans, and I often wonder how God's Spirit prevented Paul from entering certain towns. I want to awaken more to God's Spirit for guidance and trust God to direct my steps.

Write a brief prayer in the margin of page 115 asking God to make His way clear in your life and expressing your intent to yield to His Spirit.

Deference recognizes that God opens the hearts of people to His message.

Prayer seems to be a regular activity in the early church. Seeking out a place of prayer or setting aside time for prayer reveals the believers' recognition of their need for God.

Read Acts 16:11-15 and describe how Lydia became a believer in verse 14:

Lydia attended a prayer meeting and worshipped God. Paul and Silas spoke with her and several other women in Philippi, but it was the Lord who opened her heart. This reminds us that while we can pray and share the good news about Jesus, it is God who transforms hearts. We lack deference when we focus on behavior modification rather than heart change. We exercise humility and respect for God's power when we don't make ministry about us. It also takes the pressure off to yield results and allows us to embrace God's grace knowing that He is the heart-changer.

Deference is willingness to prolong physical oppression for another's spiritual freedom.

While no one can change without God's power, throughout the Book of Acts He chooses to use people to bring the message. Sometimes the delivery has seemed glamorous with supernatural wind and fire like at Pentecost (Acts 2), and other times it took the shape of one personal conversation in the desert like Philip and the Ethiopian eunuch (Acts 8). In today's passage, we find that Paul and Silas had a unique opportunity to be God's instruments of grace.

Read Acts 16:16-34 and answer the following questions:

Where were Paul and Silas headed again? (v. 16)

Who did they encounter on the way? (v. 16)

What did Paul do with regard to the girl? (v. 18)

How did this lead to a riot? (vv. 19-22)

What did Paul and Silas endure as a result? (vv. 22-24)

What were Paul and Silas doing around midnight? (v. 25)

What caused the jailer to ask for salvation? (vv. 27-30)

How did Paul answer the jailer's questions? (v. 31)

Valuing relationships over rules resulted in a change of mind about getting baptized at a new church. Another person may have felt led to make a different choice. As we awaken to God's grace, we notice He leads different people in different ways. Our responsibility is not to approve or disapprove of other's choices but instead to focus on personal worship and prayer so that we can allow the Lord to fill us with His grace and apply that grace to our personal situations.

Talk with God

Lord, deference isn't my personality type, but it is Yours. Help me to learn to yield to the Holy Spirit and consider others in my decisions. Show me when to stand up boldly and when to yield in order to remove barriers to the gospel. Awaken me to Your grace so that I can extend it to others! Amen.

Memory Verse Exercise

Read the Memory Verse on page 106 several times, and then fill in the blanks below as you recite it:

We _____ that we are all _____ the same way, by the undeserved _____ of the _____ Jesus.

(Acts 15:11)

Day 3: Grace to Keep an Open Mind

Scripture Focus

Acts 17

Big Idea

Searching the Scriptures while also keeping an open mind helps us evaluate new ideas with discernment.

As we awaken to God's grace, we might find previously held beliefs shifting. Here are three examples of how a better understanding of Scripture coupled with open-mindedness helped some women awaken to grace:

"All through the beginning of my Christian journey I listened to preachers who led me to believe that God was a genie. They quoted Scriptures like, 'I can do all things through Christ who strengthens me' and 'My God will provide all my needs according to His riches in glory.' All I had to do was submit all my wishes, and He would provide. But then I would get so frustrated when God didn't give me the things I'd pray for. As I've grown in my faith, being able to understand those Scriptures in context helped me find peace in whatever situation God has me in because I know He is in control."

"'Spare the rod, spoil the child' doesn't give you permission to beat your children. Submitting to your husband doesn't mean he can abuse you in any way. My now ex-husband used those verses out of context to abuse and control my children and me. God still loves me; I'm his beloved daughter. It took time for God to break down those walls and get that in my heart."

"Growing up I thought I was a Christian because I was a good girl. I didn't know until age twenty-nine that a Christian is not one who comes from a good family but one who believes in Jesus and commits their life to Him by faith, not works."

These examples reveal how distortions of truth can impact people. It can be painful and separate us from God and others.

Do you have an example where your beliefs shifted as you understood the Word of God better? If so, write it below:

Studying God's Word is near and dear to my heart because it contains the truth that leads us to God. He longs to transform our lives with grace and awaken us through His Word. Knowing the context and background culture, as well as following good principles of interpretation and application, are necessary so we don't misunderstand His heart behind what is written in the Bible. From the women who shared their mindset changes, we can see how others can twist Scripture to suit their own opinions. Paul took the responsibility of engaging people with God's message very seriously.

Read Acts 17:1-9 and write the verbs found in verses 2-3 below:

In the NLT the verbs were:

- went,
- used (the Scriptures),
- explained,
- proved, and
- said.

Other versions included the verb "reasoned," which was translated from the Greek word *dialegomai*, which means "to think different things with one's self, mingle thought with thought; to ponder, revolve in mind; to converse, discourse with one, argue, discuss."[15]

Extra Insight

Thessalonica was "predominantly Greek, even though it was controlled by Rome." It had some freedoms that distinguished it with an elected citizen's assembly, the ability to mint their own coins, and no Roman garrison presence.[13] It was the largest and most prosperous city of the province of Macedonia at the time, with a population of around two hundred thousand.[14]

I wonder if Paul were to take a personality assessment that we would find "thinker" on his results. In Thessalonica, Paul preached and discussed from the Old Testament Scriptures regarding Jesus's position as the Messiah. We know it takes faith to believe in Jesus, and that the Lord must open the hearts of those who hear, but reason has its place in our spiritual awakenings.

How has reason or logic played a part in your spiritual journey?

Extra Insight

We notice that Paul initiated these discussions on the Sabbath because he labored during the week as a tentmaker to earn a living (Acts 18:3; 1 Thessalonians 2:9; 2 Thessalonians 3:7-10).[16]

Reason has a falling-off point, where faith comes into play, but we don't check our brains at the door. My pastor says he walks down a long stable dock of reason before jumping off in faith at the end of it. I love how the Greek verb *dialegomai* describes how we think different things within ourselves and mingle thought with thought. This takes time, removal of distractions, and going beneath the surface to consider possibilities.

Where and when do you do your best thinking?

As I contemplated that question, I thought about moments when I'm at the gym, on a walk, praying, reading, journaling, or driving. I noticed a common thread. These are all times when I don't have a phone or screen near me. Removing distractions seems important for me to process thoughts on a deeper level.

What might be one small way you could prioritize the environment that allows you to think deeply today?

I'm writing "short walk" in my schedule for later in the day so that I can spend some focused time thinking about life, God, and all the decisions I'm currently facing. Our habits as Christ-followers help us make progress in spiritual growth. Getting intentional about making time for reflection isn't a habit I've heard taught, but in our distraction culture, it may be a new pattern we need to cultivate. Let's move on and learn some practical truths to guide our thought mingling.

Read Acts 17:10-15 and draw a line to match the current ending of each sentence. (I did the first one for you.)

A. The believers sent Paul and Barnabas to — Berea.

B. The first place they went was — the Jewish synagogue.

C. The people of Berea were more — open-minded.

D. The Bereans listened to the message and — searched the Scriptures.

E. They wanted to see if Paul and Silas were — telling the truth.

F. As a result, many Jews and Greeks — believed.

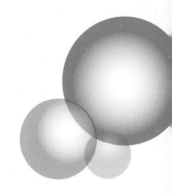

I hope you noticed a progression. The Bereans didn't immediately embrace every new idea presented. They first searched the Scriptures to see if Paul and Barnabas were telling the truth.

What can we learn and apply in our own lives from the Bereans?

Studying God's Word helps us filter the messages presented. We need the balance of an open-minded heart posture coupled with the diligence to study the Bible. This isn't just with regard to our religious doctrine. God's Word speaks to so many areas of life. It shapes our worldview, which impacts how we process our thoughts, treat people, spend our time and money, and discern truth from error.

What has been consuming your thought life lately?

With regard to what you've been thinking about, where might the Lord be calling you to:

- keep more of an open mind? (Write a few ideas here.)

Extra Insight

"The Berean synagogue searched the Scriptures, perhaps partly by communal memory and partly by means of a local Torah scroll."[17]

Answers: A. Berea, B. the Jewish synagogue; C. open-minded D. searched the Scriptures; E. telling the truth. F. believed.

Week 4   121

- search the Scriptures for guidance? (What does the Bible say on this topic?)

I've been thinking about recent events and how divided Christians seem at times. I want to listen with an open mind but also study the Bible to gain clarity. I also think a lot about my children and their choices. Figuring out my role as less of an authority and more of an advisor gives me much to ponder on any given day.

We need an open mind and God's Word so that we don't become short-sighted. Paul wrote a letter to the church at Ephesus encouraging the believers to exercise discernment: "We won't be tossed and blown about by every wind of new teaching. We will not be influenced when people try to trick us with lies so clever they sound like the truth" (Ephesians 4:14). Yet we don't want to be like some of the Thessalonian Jews who lacked the Bereans' openness to consider the gospel message. They followed Paul and Silas to Berea to stir up trouble just like they had done in Thessalonica. Paul then went on to Athens and sent for Silas and Timothy later.

Read Acts 17:16-34 and summarize how Paul used his own creativity and open-mindedness to relate the gospel to the Athenians:

I love how Paul knew His message so well but also sought to know his audience. He crafted his message in a way that would be relevant to his listeners. I noticed:

- Paul observed his surroundings. (He *was deeply troubled by the idols he saw.*)
- He looked for something to affirm. (He *complimented their deeply religious beliefs.*)
- He connected with the culture as a springboard for the gospel. (He *used an idol and quoted poetry from their Athenian culture to hook their attention so he could talk about Jesus.*)
- Paul boldly corrected their idolatry with the truth about God. (He *didn't hold back in telling them of their need to repent and a day of judgment to come.*)

Of all these methods, put a star next to the one that most resonates with you today. We can learn from Paul how to use the minds God gave us to present the gospel in our culture with clarity and thoughtfulness. He didn't shy away from culture but used it as a catalyst to connect the message of Christ. We've seen this pattern throughout Acts.

Extra Insight

"When Paul came to Athens, it had long since lost its empire and wealth. Its population probably numbered no more than ten thousand. Yet it had a glorious past on which it continued to live."[18]

- For a Jewish crowd in Antioch Pisidia, Paul presented the gospel using the Hebrew Scriptures, which would have been familiar to them. (Acts 13)
- When in Lystra, Paul spoke with the peasants living in the countryside using nature as a touchpoint. (Acts 14)
- In Athens, he used local literature and idols to boldly proclaim Christ. (Acts 17)

Paul put into practice what he wrote to the church at Corinth about his desire to "be all things to all men" so that he might win some for the sake of the gospel (1 Corinthians 9:20-22).

What are some ways you have seen people consider their audience and make cultural connections to share the truth about God?

Several years ago, when I was substitute teaching in a local high school, I kept hearing students reference a series of novels. While the books were fantasy, the topics evoked conversations about good and evil, afterlife, and issues of morality. I decided to read the series so that I could join the conversation. At the time some Christians spoke out publicly against these books—a position I respect—but I saw a way to use them as a launching pad for gospel conversations.

We need a firm grasp on the Scriptures so that we carefully apply Paul's lessons on open-mindedness from Acts 17. Paul used pagan literature and even idols to help his audience connect to his message, but he was careful not to become attached to that literature or idolatry. We have awakened to freedom, but we use that freedom to serve one another, not to indulge in ungodliness (Galatians 5:13).

Daily Wrap-Up

What is one way you noticed God at work in Acts 17?

How did God's people respond?

Some people embraced Paul's message while others stirred up a mob or laughed in contempt. Those who believed found life and purpose while those who didn't missed out on a personal relationship with their Creator. Keeping an open mind had immense impact on Paul's second missionary journey, and it can greatly change the course of our lives as well.

Today we focused on this truth: *searching the Scriptures while also keeping an open mind helps us evaluate new ideas with discernment.*

How would you summarize your personal takeaway from today's lesson?

We saw Paul use his intellect in reasoning, preaching, and relating to culture with one goal in mind. He longed for all people to awaken to God's grace in their lives. He knew that "in him we live and move and exist" (Acts 17:28). Without Him, we search for lesser gods to meet our longings. The more we awaken to His grace, the more open-minded and intentional we can be in sharing His message with others.

Talk with God

Lord, I know I have so much more to learn. Help me to see any blind spots that require open-mindedness or more diligent study of Your Word. Lead me by Your Spirit so that I might know the truth and share it with others. Keep awakening me to Your grace and help me apply it in my life today. Amen.

Memory Verse Exercise

Read the Memory Verse on page 106 several times, and then fill in the blanks below as you recite it:

We _____ that _____ are all _____ the same way, _____ the undeserved _____ of the _____ Jesus.

(Acts 15:11)

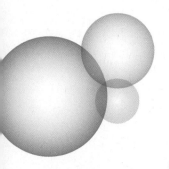

Day 4: Partners in Grace

Scripture Focus

Acts 18

Big Idea

We can awaken more fully to God's grace when we surround ourselves with godly friends.

Our youth pastor recently preached at my church asking people to evaluate their squad. By "squad" he meant the people you are doing life with and who are shaping you. He mentioned how parents love when he teaches their students that "bad company corrupts good character" (1 Corinthians 15:33). He reminded the listeners that Scripture applies to everyone—including adults. It's not enough to have good theology, habits, and character. Scripture teaches the importance of good friends so we should find our squad carefully.

In Acts we've seen the disciples of Jesus preach the gospel to a variety of people in a variety of settings. Some believed and others didn't. Jesus taught us to love and serve everyone, especially those who are far from God. Yet when it comes to those closest to you—your squad—they should be Christians who love God and others and help you love God and others.

Paul wasn't alone in his pursuit of Christ. He surrounded himself with godly friends. He understood his need to have like-minded friends and mentor others. He lived out Proverbs 13:20, "Walk with the wise and become wise; associate with fools and get in trouble."

Who is on your current squad? (Who are you doing life with and listening to?) List the people who come to mind right away.

These are the people with whom we spend the most time. My three included my husband, sister, and closest friend. Today we'll look through the lens of friendship to see what we can learn from Paul's squad as he completes his second missionary journey.

Read Acts 18:1-3 and identify the two new friends Paul made in Corinth:

P_____   A_____

We know that Paul came to Corinth with a heavy heart since he wrote in 1 Corinthians, "I came to you in weakness—timid and trembling" (1 Corinthians 2:3). He had experienced many trials, including separation from his ministry partners, Silas and Timothy. He likely was distressed over the state of the new believers in Thessalonica who were persecuted.

Paul found common ground with Priscilla and Aquila. This husband-and-wife team shared not only his faith but also his trade as a tentmaker. As we continue to study Acts, we will find that these new friends became dear to Paul. We never want to get to a point where we believe we've met our relationship quota. We need new people, and new people need us.

As you consider the truth that new friends can become dear friends, who is someone new in your life whom you might reach out to this week?

With technology, it can be tempting to connect with those who have known us for years instead of seeking out new relationships. When we moved a few years ago, I found starting over more challenging than I expected. It was easier to call, FaceTime, and text with my old friends who had known me for decades than pursue new relationships. While I'm not giving up my dear old friends, I'm finding new treasures as I invite women into my life for prayer, accountability, and friendship.

Friends and ministry partners can also come alongside and help us in tangible ways.

How do we see this truth played out in Acts 18:4-8?

Extra Insight

Paul wrote 1 and 2 Thessalonians during his time in Corinth on this second missionary journey.

When a mob threatened Paul, he was sent away for safety, while Silas and Timothy remained behind to continue their work. They weren't with him in Athens (Acts 17:14) but rejoined him in Corinth (Acts 18:5). Once they arrived, they brought much-needed encouragement and tangible help that allowed him to devote more time to preaching. Perhaps this was due to the good report regarding the Thessalonian believers (1 Thessalonians 3:6) as well as the monetary gift they brought from the church at Philippi (2 Corinthians 11:9; Philippians 4:14-15). His friends bolstered Paul both emotionally and financially. Luke does not always present the human element of Paul's state of mind in Acts, but the letters he wrote from the cities on his journey help us to fill in the gaps to remember that he sometimes felt anxious or frustrated.

His friends' arrival freed him to focus on preaching. This ministry brought many challenges, but it was God's call on Paul's life. As a result of his friends coming alongside him, many people in Corinth became believers and were baptized.

Depending on your current situation, choose to answer one of the following two questions:

- **If you are feeling overwhelmed with many ministry tasks, what friends can you invite to help?**

- **If you are feeling some margin in your schedule, who is a godly person you know who might need some assistance to do what God has called him/her to do?**

I've been so blessed by my friend Tanya. She has strengthened me with practical help but also fervent prayer. If you aren't sure what to do to help someone in ministry, a first step might be to pray for them. Then ask God to show you ways that you can be a partner in grace.

Prayer will be a continual theme as we awaken to God in everyday life. While God gives us friends as gifts, we can never lose sight of the truth that Jesus is our closest friend.

Read Acts 18:9-17 and write the words that Jesus spoke to Paul in verses 9-10 below:

We need friends to encourage us, but God Himself longs to be closest. He may not speak in a vision in the night like He did with Paul, but His Word is full of truths that reveal His heart for us. God sent His Son, Jesus, so that our relationship with Him could be restored. Through the blood of Christ, we can draw near to God. He gives us access to Him in prayer. Just as He was with Paul, He is with us.

Write your name in the blanks below to personalize the truths He spoke to Paul and bring them a little closer to home:

_____ Don't be afraid!

Speak out! Don't be silent! _____

For I am with you _____

We need a squad, but even more we need God. He is the friend who sticks closer than a brother (Proverbs 18:24). Close friends are important so we should find our few carefully, but God may ask us to move or leave our group. Paul stayed in Corinth for a year and a half. He developed relationships and put down roots. Yet when the Lord called him to move on, Paul followed God's lead only taking his new friends Priscilla and Aquila along. And he parted with them after the first leg of the journey.

Read Acts 18:18-23 and trace the path on the map below starting in Corinth and ending at Antioch either with your finger or pen: (These are legs 6, 7, 8, and 9.) Then write P and A under the word *Ephesus* since Priscilla and Aquila stayed there:

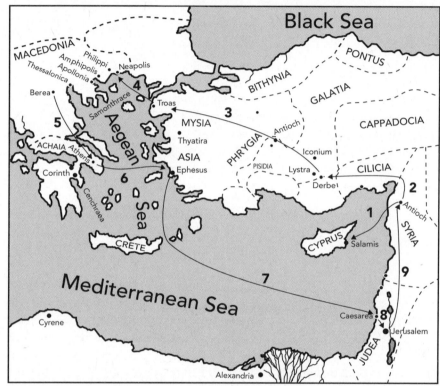

Paul traveled from AD 49–52 on this second missionary trip. Who were some of the friends you can recall who were with him at different points on his journey?

Perhaps you thought of Silas, Timothy, Jason, Priscilla, Aquila, or others. None of these people were with him on the first missionary journey so Paul learned to make new friends. He also kept up with old friends through letter writing. From the letters he wrote to churches and individuals, we know that Paul was not just a gospel preacher and church planter but also a friend-maker. He valued people, but at the end of the day, he never allowed his friendships to prevent him from obeying the Lord.

If God has ever led you away from people (because of geography or conflict), what were some of the challenges you faced?

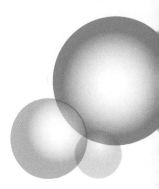

How did you see God's grace at work in the midst of it?

Maybe you weren't able to answer that question, but someday the Lord may call you to move. Changing squads can be difficult, but holding people loosely and God tightly will help prepare us. My single adult son just moved to a new city in another state, and the adjustment has brought periods of loneliness. New friendships take time, and we all long to be known. Yet when the Lord calls us away, we must be willing to go where God leads even if it separates us from dear friends.

While Paul was traveling to Antioch, his new friends Priscilla and Aquila stayed in Ephesus. From their time in Ephesus, we learn that friends are also willing to correct as well as support each other.

Read Acts 18:24-28 and write below one thing you noticed about how Priscilla and Aquila treated Apollos:

I appreciate how they admonished him but took him aside privately. Apollos could have felt prideful about his knowledge and eloquence as a speaker. This might have made it difficult for him to receive criticism. Instead, we see God using him in powerful ways as he continued to grow in grace. We may know the Scriptures well, like Apollos, or be new to studying God's Word, but we all can grow in understanding the way of God with greater accuracy. This means we need to be teachable and allow our friends to sharpen us.

Who is someone in your life whom you could invite/or have invited to speak truth in your life?

I told you earlier about my encouraging, helpful friend Tanya. She could also be called Truthful Tanya. I appreciate that when she has something to share, she'll ask this question, "Are you up for some sandpaper right now, or do you need a warm blanket?" I never want to hear the sandpaper, but I know I need it. I've given her permission to lovingly let me know when I have a blind spot. It may not always feel good in the moment, but gracious friends speak the truth in love for our benefit.

Daily Wrap-Up

What is one way you noticed God at work in Acts 18?

How did God's people respond?

The Lord spoke directly to Paul with words of encouragement, and He provided friends along the route of ministry. Paul responded with a willingness to move, even when it meant leaving behind people whom he loved.

Today we focused on this truth: *we can awaken more fully to God's grace when we surround ourselves with godly friends.*

How would you summarize your personal takeaway from today's lesson?

It's been said that "you are the sum of the five people closest to you." Whether or not that is exactly true, we are impacted by our squad. We want to pursue relationships that lead us closer to Christ, but we also want to hold those friendships loosely so that we are willing to let go as God leads.

Talk with God

Lord, show me where to invest in relationships. Lead me to new friends who need encouragement and help. Help me to surround myself with voices that point me to You. Soften my heart to listen to correction so that I can grow stronger in my faith. Show me where and when to release people in order to more fully follow Your lead. Amen.

Memory Verse Exercise

Read the Memory Verse on page 106 several times, and then fill in the blanks below as you recite it:

We _____ that _____ _____ all _____ the same way, _____ the undeserved _____ of the _____ _____.

(Acts 15:11)

Day 5: The Eyes of Grace

Scripture Focus

Acts 19

Big Idea

We need eyes to see God's grace in exposing spiritual realities.

During my second pregnancy, my husband and I found out we were having a girl. Our son was three years old at the time, and I went into planning mode. I gathered girl clothes from friends, prepared the nursery, and anticipated the arrival of Sara Abigail.

Somewhere in the third trimester, I decided I loved the name Abigail so much that I didn't want to use it for a middle name. My husband's sister is named Sara so I promised my husband that we would use it for a future girl because I wanted to name this daughter Abigail. We both had no idea how soon we would be able to use both names.

Ten days before they were born, we found out during a routine appointment that I was carrying twins. At my previous ultrasound, my husband and my doctor—who attended our church—had been discussing the current church building project while occasionally pointing out a baby organ on the screen. I needed another ultrasound later in my pregnancy because of how big my stomach was measuring, and I went to that appointment alone. It was then my doctor noticed a second baby! They had both been there all along, but this ultrasound with an undistracted physician exposed the reality that both Sara Grace and Abigail Hope were on their way into the world. I see God's gracious hand in gifting us with two daughters when we were expecting only one.

As you reflect on your life, where have you encountered God's grace in unexpected places or situations?

Perhaps a devasting job loss turned into a new career pursuit. Maybe a health challenge drew you near to God in ways you couldn't have anticipated. Sometimes relationship difficulties can propel us to see blessings we had previously missed.

Awakening to God in everyday life through the Book of Acts hasn't changed my circumstances, but it has changed the lens I use to view them. This week we've focused on awakening to God's grace. We've seen believers exercise grace to disagree, show deference, keep an open mind, and recognize God's gift of grace in friends and ministry partners.

Today we'll find that God's grace awakens us in unexpected places and might unsettle the way we've always done things. Unsettling can be a positive state as we learn to trust God even through seasons of ambiguity. In Acts 19, we'll see that God loves people so much that He graciously brings spiritual realities to the surface.

We'll notice that God:

- opens our eyes for fuller understanding,
- opens our eyes to the need for a spiritual bonfire (you might be raising your eyebrows at this one, but hang with me—the Scripture will bring us clarity), and
- opens our eyes to see cultural counterfeits.

Read Acts 19:1-7 and describe how God exposed a need for fuller understanding:

Extra Insight

Mark 1:8 reminds us that John's baptism was one of repentance rather than salvation. John was speaking of Jesus when he said, "I baptize you with water, but he will baptize you with the Holy Spirit!"

This first segment of Paul's third missionary journey doesn't teach a second work of the Holy Spirit but revealed the need for clarity. John's message couldn't save people but instead prepared them to receive the truth about Jesus. Christ alone has the power to save and initiate the indwelling of the Holy Spirit.

Just as Apollos in Acts 18 needed more accuracy in his understanding about Jesus, these twelve men found God's grace when their eyes were opened to fuller revelation.

Can you think of a time when a message, book, or friend provided information to give you a more complete view on a spiritual topic? (If so, write the topic below.)

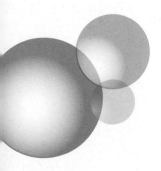

Books written about Acts help me understand the culture of the original audience. Feedback from a group of women helps me shape the content of my writing. When our eyes are opened to areas of concern, we can find the power to change. If we don't submit to gentle correction, our lessons can sometimes come in more severe ways. Seven sons of a leading priest learned this very personally in Ephesus.

Read Acts 19:8-22 and circle the letter that best completes these statements:

1. Paul preached boldly for three months about the kingdom of God first in the:

A. Town square

B. Synagogue

C. Riverbank prayer meeting

2. People became stubborn and rejected his message so Paul took the believers with him and for two years he preached at:

A. The lecture hall of Tyrannus

B. The statue of Artemis

C. The house churches

3. When the seven sons of Sceva used Jesus's name in their incantation, the evil spirit:

A. Went away

B. Didn't speak

C. Overpowered them, attacked them with violence, leaving them naked and battered

4. This incident led people to:

A. Honor the name of Jesus

B. Confess their sinful practices and become believers

C. Burn their sorcery books in a public bonfire

D. All of the above

5. Paul sent these two assistants ahead to Macedonia:

A. Barnabas and John Mark

B. Timothy and Erastus

C. Silas and Apollos

As you read these verses, how did you see counterfeits exposed?

Extra Insight

"The hall of Tyrannus was probably a lecture room or school building, and Tyrannus was the owner or the teacher." Tyrannus means "tyrant" so it might have been a nickname.[23]

The seven sons of Sceva used Jesus's name but didn't have a personal relationship with Him. People during this time in history made a living practicing exorcism and would call on the name of any and every god, reciting a long list of names and hoping they found the right one that would work.[24] These seven brothers likely heard about Paul's successful miracles using Jesus's name and so they said, "I command you in the name of Jesus, whom Paul preaches, to come out!" (Acts 19:13b).

They left the incident naked and afraid, with a greater understanding that the power in Jesus's name can't come through a proxy. As a result, many feared God, believed in Jesus, and held a book burning. The cost of these books would have been the equivalent of around a million dollars in today's currency.

With the power of Jesus, the new believers didn't need the incantations, potions, and spells found in these expensive books. They now believed in God's grace rather than sorcery. Likely you and I don't have a closet filled with valuable magic books to burn in our firepits, but I wonder if we have some things that might need to be tossed in a spiritual bonfire.

Take a moment and ask the Lord to graciously open your eyes to any habits, sinful practices, or items that your life would be better without. Write a brief prayer and anything you sense from the Holy Spirit below:

There was a time in my life when gossip had crept into my day-to-day conversations, particularly as I chatted on the phone. My husband noticed and mentioned it to me. Instead of addressing it, I made sure I was out of his earshot when I gossiped. I rationalized and justified my bad habit for way too long. As the Lord graciously opened my eyes, I recognized my need to repent. We don't want to be legalist and shaming, but we do want to recognize and eliminate anything that is dragging us down rather than lifting us up spiritually.

If something comes to your mind that fits in the spiritual hindrance category in your life, write it on a small piece of paper and then light a match and burn it. Sometimes a tactile gesture like this can help mark our desire to follow Jesus wholeheartedly. This is a symbolic action rather than any sort of magical ritual, a physical reminder of a spiritual change.

A spiritual bonfire can seem inconvenient or unnecessary, but its light and heat remind us to stay away from harmful practices. We might be tempted to think that our small initiatives don't matter that much. Maybe what came to mind for you seemed insignificant—like scrolling social media too much or dwelling on negative thoughts—or perhaps what you want to overcome seems huge and insurmountable. Either way, imagine how your life could change if you were able to make real progress in this area. God longs to graciously empower us to grow and will supply the power we need to relegate hindrances to the burn pile.

Faithfulness in small acts of obedience is exactly what we see happening in Acts 19 with powerful results. Acts 19:20 says, "So the message about the Lord spread widely and had a powerful effect." New believers in Jesus put to death the old things in their lives to make way for God to work. But not everyone rejoiced in these changes taking place in Ephesus.

Read Acts 19:23-41 and summarize in a sentence why Demetrius and his fellow craftsmen started a riot:

When people began to believe the message about Jesus, it affected the profits of those making money on counterfeits. Believing in God's grace through faith in Christ meant believers had no need for statues depicting false gods. The silversmiths and other craftsmen depended on respect for Artemis to sell their wares.

They gathered, organized, and rioted to keep their false messages alive. The picture in Acts 19 is one of confusion as Paul's friends Gaius and Aristarchus were dragged into the amphitheater. Faith in Jesus can also upset the cultural lies of our day.

Where do you notice unrest and confusion in our world today? (There are so many ways to answer this—just jot down one or two that stand out to you.)

Even as God's message was boldly preached with miraculous healings and widespread repentance, the enemy still attempted to sow confusion and opposition. We don't have shrines to Artemis today, but commentators suggest she was a mixture of the Greek goddess of the hunt and the Asian goddess of fertility and banking.[26] People today still hunt for prosperity, beauty, sex, and all sorts of counterfeit gods. Sharing the good news about Christ can't help exposing the emptiness of those pursuits.

Write a brief prayer below for whatever area of confusion you identified in the previous question. Ask God to graciously intervene and reveal Himself through the situation:

Daily Wrap-Up

What is one way you noticed God at work in Acts 19?

Extra Insight

A build-up of silt was affecting the Ephesian port and in turn its commercial capabilities. "At the time of Paul's arrival, the people of Ephesus, while surrounded by signs of past wealth and still enjoying many of its fruits, were becoming conscious of the precariousness of their position as a commercial and political center of Asia and were turning more toward the temple of Artemis in support of their economy."[25]

How did God's people respond?

God used His people and His power to awaken people to His grace. He did this by exposing areas of lack and shaking up traditionally held views. He does this in our lives as well when He:

- opens our eyes where we need fuller understanding,
- opens our eyes to our need for a spiritual bonfire, or
- opens our eyes to cultural counterfeits.

Today we focused on this truth: *we need eyes to see God's grace in exposing spiritual realities.*

How would you summarize your personal takeaway from today's lesson?

I'm continuing to ask the Lord to show me where I need a spiritual bonfire. I want to let go of anything that is hindering me from awakening to God in my everyday life. I'm so glad that we don't have to live like the sons of Sceva with a secondhand relationship with Jesus. We can keep growing and learning as He leads us with truth and grace.

Talk with God

Lord, awaken me to see my surroundings with Your eyes. Give me vision to identify where I need to grow in truth and grace. Reveal areas where sin is holding me back. I want to take seriously what You take seriously. Remind me of the spiritual war happening all around me. Thank You that I don't have to go through a person to get to You. Help me to make sense of the opposition I see in the world and sort through the confusion with Your wisdom. Amen.

Memory Verse Exercise

Read the Memory Verse on page 106 several times, and then fill in the blanks below as you recite it:

We _____ _____ ____ ____ all _____ the _____ way,

____ the _____ _____ of ____ _____ _____.

(Acts 15:11)

Weekly Wrap-Up

Review the Big Idea for each day, and then write any personal application that comes to mind.

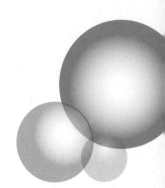

Day 1: Grace to Disagree

Big Idea: because believers don't agree on everything, we need God's grace to work through our varying viewpoints.

Personal Application:_____

_____

Day 2: Grace to Show Deference

Big Idea: awakening to God's grace results in valuing relationships over rules.

Personal Application:_____

_____

Day 3: Grace to Keep an Open Mind

Big Idea: searching the Scriptures while also keeping an open mind helps us evaluate new ideas with discernment.

Personal Application:_____

_____

Day 4: Partners in Grace

Big Idea: we can awaken more fully to God's grace when we surround ourselves with godly friends.

Personal Application:_____

_____

Day 5: The Eyes of Grace

Big Idea: we need eyes to see God's grace in exposing spiritual realities.

Personal Application:_____

_____

Video Viewer Guide: Week 4

John 17:20

God wants us to give _____ to _____ knowing sometimes _____ will be the ones in need of it.

We can awaken to grace in _____.

Acts 15: 1-2

Acts 15: 4-12

Acts 15: 13-19

Four ways to handle disagreements:

• _____ to _____

• Really _____

• _____ _____

• Consult the _____

Acts 15:36-41

_____ when necessary.

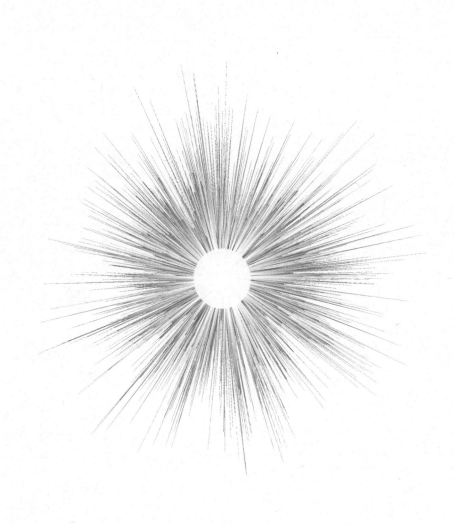

Week 5

Awakening to God's Mission

Acts 20–24

Memory Verse

But my life is worth nothing to me unless I use it for finishing the work assigned me by the Lord Jesus—the work of telling others the Good News about the wonderful grace of God.

(Acts 20:24)

Day 1: A Mission Worth the Sacrifices

Many meaningful pursuits in my life have been accompanied by sacrifices. Raising children included sleepless nights from crying newborns. Attempting to stay in good health required a pattern of scheduling meal plans and exercise. Pursuing deep friendships sometimes meant attending girls' nights or other social gatherings when this introvert would rather stay home. Most accomplishments cannot be attained without sacrifices attached.

I'm guessing that you also have sacrificed time, energy, money, and relationships for purposes you strongly support. What challenges have you experienced associated with a calling or cause that is near to your heart?

Maybe you thought of working, parenting, adoption, feeding the homeless, caring for an elderly person, teaching, or any number of other pursuits. For those who consider themselves disciples of Christ, we share a common mission that also requires sacrifice. Let's remind ourselves of Scripture's definition of this mission before we discuss the costs associated with it. Jesus outlined His command in a passage of Scripture often referred to as the Great Commission.

Read Matthew 28:18-20 below and summarize the instructions He gave:

"Jesus came and told his disciples, 'I have been given all authority in heaven and on earth. Therefore, go and make disciples of all the nations, baptizing them in the name of the Father and the Son and the Holy Spirit. Teach these new disciples to obey all the commands I have given you. And be sure of this: I am with you always, even to the end of the age.'"

(Matthew 28:18-20)

Big Idea

Sharing the good news can present challenges in our lives, but remembering the eternal impact of the mission realigns our perspective.

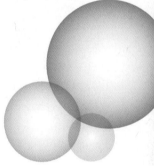

Jesus said He would be with us as we:

- make disciples,
- baptize disciples, and
- teach disciples.

The word *disciple* is associated with a learner. It is one who follows the "precepts and instructions" of another. Christians are learners who are following the teachings of Christ. How the Lord calls us to live out His mission of making, baptizing, and teaching new learners can be lived out in a variety of ways.[1]

Up to this point in Acts, we've often found the church gathering on Saturdays in the pattern of Judaism's Sabbath. Scholar William Willimon notes the gathering in Acts 20:7 as "one of the New Testament's earliest definite references to weekly *Sunday worship*." This shows the progression of Christianity as a distinct entity from Judaism with its own particular day of worship.[3]

In Acts 20 the pronouns change to "us" and "we" because Luke is now part of the group so he is recording information firsthand.[4]

The apostle Paul traveled, preached, and equipped church leaders. As we read about Paul's journey this week, I'm praying the Lord will help you gain clarity regarding your personal call to God's mission. As we've been tracking with Paul through his missionary trips, we've noticed that everything hasn't been easy.

Here is a list of some of Paul's challenges:

- Murderous threats in Damascus (Acts 9:23) and Jerusalem (Acts 9:29).
- A mob chasing him out of town in Antioch in Pisidia (Acts 13:50).
- A mob plotting to stone him in Iconium (Acts 14:5).
- Being left for dead after being stoned in Lystra (Acts 14:19).
- Sharp disagreement with Barnabas (Acts 15:36-41).
- Hiding out from men trying to kill him in Thessalonica (Acts 17:5) and then in Berea (Acts 17:13).
- Brought before the governor for judgment in Corinth (Acts 18:12).

Some of Paul's struggles may seem foreign to your experiences, but he was human just like you and me. He got weary, struggled in relationships, and had to overcome discouragement. Even after enduring all of these trials, Paul kept on traveling around telling people about God's love and the need to turn from sin.

Read Acts 20:1-12. Describe a few of the situations faced by Paul:

Paul often had to change his travel plans because of dangerous opposition to the gospel. He believed his mission was worth making sacrifices so he embraced flexibility. He also was willing to sacrifice food and sleep to keep preaching. I love how the story of Eutychus reminds us of the humanity of the early believers. Lights flickered, people got sleepy, and even Paul's preaching couldn't prevent a little closing of the eyes to rest. Greek scholar I. Howard Marshall says the words used to describe Eutychus put him in the age range of a lad between eight and fourteen years of age.[5] After his fall, the group of believers finally got to eat the Lord's Supper. In our fast-food culture, I appreciate how the church patiently waited, giving priority to Paul's parting words even more than food.

After they ate, Paul kept preaching until dawn. People needed to be saved, and believers needed to be strengthened with the Word of God. It was worth sacrificing sleep and food to hear eternal truths.

Even though I know the gospel, sometimes familiarity can be the enemy of wonder. I want to awaken afresh to the importance of the mission—people need to know the good news about a God who loves them so they can turn from their sin and turn to God. Only God can change hearts, but He has commissioned us to go into all the world and share His message so that people can respond to it.

If you consider yourself a follower of Christ, what are some challenges you have faced either in the past or present as you heeded Jesus's call to make disciples?

I struggle with becoming forgetful, apathetic, or distracted with other tasks so that the mission of spreading God's love becomes secondary in my life. Paul seemed very focused. He was willing not only to delay eating and stay up late but also to say goodbye to people he loved in order to share the message with others.

Read Acts 20:13-27 and answer the following questions:

Where was Paul in a hurry to go? (v. 16)

Whom did he ask to come and meet him? (v. 17)

What did Paul endure that caused him many tears? (v. 19)

What was the one message Paul preached to both Jews and Greeks? (v. 21)

What did Paul say was most important to him? (v. 24)

Why did Paul say that anyone suffering eternal death would not be his fault? (vv. 26-27)

After reading this account, what inspires you from Paul's mindset?

How would you fill in the blank, "But my life is worth nothing to me unless I use it for _____."

I want my life to honor God. Sometimes my head gets so wrapped around earthly concerns like health, finances, home management, and earthly relationships that I lose sight of the eternal reality that every person will die and face judgment. Paul didn't want anyone to suffer eternal death because He failed to present God's message. Studying Acts is awakening me to the priority of God's mission. I hope it's awakening you in a similar way!

Paul loved the Ephesian elders, but he was willing to part with them so that others might hear the good news. In his closing remarks, Paul took off his evangelist hat and put on a pastoral one.

Read Acts 20:28-38 and circle the numbers of the statements below that reflect Paul's final words:

1. Guard yourselves and God's people.

2. Be judgmental and critical of God's people.

3. Feed and shepherd God's flock.

4. The Holy Spirit has appointed you as leaders.

5. Watch out for those who have radical faith in Jesus.

6. Watch out for false teachers.

7. I entrust you to God and the message of His grace.

8. Jesus said, "It is more blessed to give than to receive."

Together they knelt, prayed, cried, embraced, and kissed goodbye. Paul had devoted three years to the Ephesian church and these leaders. He loved them, and they loved him. Yet they parted knowing they would never see each other again because the gospel mission took priority over everything else.

Paul wanted the Ephesian elders to have the mindset of giving more than receiving. Today's lesson has focused on the sacrifices associated with fulfilling God's mission.

What is one sacrifice the Lord might be calling you to make in your everyday life to bring love and truth to others?

If you weren't sure how to answer this question, take some time to pray and ask God to show you a pathway to making sacrifices in a way that impacts His kingdom.

Daily Wrap-Up

What is one way you noticed God at work in Acts 20?

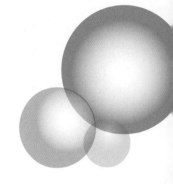

How did the believers respond?

God led Paul on his journey and used Him to revive a fallen boy and encourage church leaders along the way. The people responded by listening to Paul's teaching and accepting the sacrifice of separation that accompanied Paul's mission.

We can learn from the early church to normalize the hardships that accompany serving God. He never promised it would be easy, but the Lord does promise to lead and comfort us. We see His Spirit at work in Paul's life, and we can awaken to Him in ours.

Today we focused on this truth: *sharing the good news can present challenges in our lives, but remembering the eternal impact of the mission realigns our perspective.*

How would you summarize your personal takeaway from today's lesson?

Difficulties and opposition aren't usually fun, and we can lament the pain they cause. Yet when we focus on the lives that can be transformed by the gospel message, we can more easily endure the challenges.

Talk with God

Lord, stamp eternity in my eyes so that I can see what matters most. Give me an urgency to share Your message but help me to do it in step with Your Spirit. I don't want to shove information down other people's throats but instead invite them to know You. Show me what that looks like in my life today. I want to share Your love with others, but I don't always know how. I'm willing—please lead me. Amen.

Memory Verse Exercise

Read the Memory Verse on page 140 several times, and then fill in the blanks below as you recite it:

But my _____ is worth nothing to me unless I use it for

_____ the work assigned me by the Lord _____—

the work of telling others the _____ News about the wonderful

_____ of God.

(Acts 20:24)

Day 2: Misunderstanding and the Mission

Scripture Focus

Acts 21

Big Idea

We can follow God's leading in our lives without expecting everyone around us to understand our plans, methods, or motives.

I remember trembling with a hot cup of tea in my hands in the coffee shop as I waited for the others to arrive. They had been close friends for many years until we had a falling out over things that happened in our church.

Their families had all left the church, and I hadn't seen some of them in months. I wasn't sure about the motives of the woman who invited us all, but I suspected she wanted to see if we could reunite after the dust of the incident had settled. We caught up on what was going on in our lives, but it ended up being the final attempt made to move past our differences.

One of the hardest parts for me in all of it related to being misunderstood. From my perspective, several of them had written a first draft in their head of what I was thinking and feeling, and that became their truth. When we talked about the church situation, whatever I said didn't seem to matter because they had already written the script. Nothing I added changed their narrative so the misunderstandings couldn't be cleared up.

Can you think of a time when you felt misunderstood? If so, write about it below:

Maybe others didn't know what it was like to parent your children, be married to your spouse, work at your job, or live in your neighborhood, so they couldn't fully appreciate all that went into the decisions you made. Perhaps today, you and I can both relate to the apostle Paul because he was misunderstood by friends and foes. Yet in the midst of others' opinions, he declared that he was ready to do whatever it took for God's will to be done in his life.

Read Acts 21:1-14 and answer the following questions:

What did the local believers in Tyre say that Paul should not do? (v. 4)

How did Agabus act out what would happen to Paul? (v. 11)

What did the local believers beg Paul not to do? (v. 12)

Summarize Paul's response by filling in the blank:

I am ready _____ **(v. 13)**

What statement did the believers then make? (v. 14)

Some could argue that Paul wasn't being responsible since other believers cautioned him as they listened to the Holy Spirit. Yet Warren Wiersbe pointed out that in the Greek language the words weren't prohibitive but warnings.[7] Paul had others telling him what they thought God wanted him to do.

Can you think of a situation when other people didn't support the direction you sensed God leading you? If so, give an example below:

Perhaps you wanted to start a ministry but friends thought you should focus on your family. Maybe you sensed God leading you to move to a new a town, but others didn't understand why you would ever leave them. Paul's companions could point to the guidance of the Holy Spirit combined with human reasoning regarding him traveling to Jerusalem. Yet Paul didn't allow other people to sideline his obedience to God. We can learn from him, but also from his audience. After they voiced their concerns, they ultimately said, "The Lord's will be done" (Acts 21:14).

If someone in your life is making decisions you disagree with, briefly describe the situation below:

Extra Insights

Philip probably founded the church in Caesarea and is described as *the evangelist,* "which may be meant to distinguish him from Philip the apostle."[6]

Philip's prophetic daughters were described as unmarried, which "usually referred to prepubescent or young adolescent virgins....Together with the now older male prophet Agabus...they illustrate that the Spirit of prophecy is for old and young alike."[8]

Several commentators mentioned that Agabus's display was reminiscent of the antics of many Old Testament prophets.[9]

This has been a constant struggle with my adult-ish children. Sometimes I want to control their choices when I need to allow my children to develop their own dependence on the Lord. It can be difficult to watch people we love make choices that may seem unwise in our eyes. We can share our concerns like Paul's friends did, but ultimately, we need to allow others to follow God without judgment from us.

When someone is overtly sinning against us, Jesus gave steps for correcting them in Matthew 18:15-17. This was not what was happening with Paul in Acts 21. He wasn't sinning. He just made choices with his own life that others cautioned him against. Decisions about whether you should travel somewhere, how many children you should have, or how you should spend your time or money aren't one-size-fits-all. These are wisdom issues, not sin issues.

When it comes to these decisions, the directions God leads believers may differ, depending on His individual plan for them. If we disagree, we can learn these principles from the early Christians:

1. Voice our concerns regarding what the Holy Spirit is telling us.
2. Pray for God's will to be done in their life.
3. Stop trying to enforce our opinion and trust our fellow believers to make the best decisions.

How do you think implementing these principles could impact relationships among believers today? (whether online or in person)

We can't eliminate all problems, but I believe we could prevent some relational conflicts if we practiced these steps. Paul stood up to his friends in order to follow the Lord, but let's not forget that God's prophecies always come true. Paul found trouble waiting for him in Jerusalem, just as his fellow believers said he would.

Read Acts 21:15-25 and draw a line to finish the sentence correctly:

A. Paul and the other believers stayed in the home of (v. 16)   praised God

B. In Jerusalem, Paul met with the elders and (v. 18)   Temple

C. After Paul gave his report the believers (v. 20)   James

D. James asked Paul to go to the (v. 24)   Mnason

Again, we find a misunderstanding. Paul didn't require the Gentile Christians to practice Judaism, but he didn't discourage Jewish believers from keeping their traditions. In order to clear up the misinterpretation, Paul went to the Temple to take part in a Jewish practice associated with purification.

Paul could have protested that he didn't need to prove anything, but instead he listened and did what was necessary to straighten out the confusion he hadn't caused. This gives us another insight into handling mix-ups: *we can try to clear up misunderstandings with our actions.* Unfortunately, our attempts don't always produce the outcomes we desire.

Paul did what James and the elders asked him to do, but instead of settling the crowd, his actions ignited more misunderstanding.

Read Acts 21:26-40 and briefly describe in a sentence or two what happened to Paul:

The Temple contained a wall separating the court of Gentiles from the other courts. No Gentile was allowed to go past a four-foot-high stone wall[10] with a sign posted in both Greek and Latin[11] stating the clear prohibition with the threat of death for any caught crossing the boundary.[12]

The Jews prejudged Paul as one who disregarded Jewish tradition because of his ministry to the Gentiles. Because they had seen Paul earlier in the day with a Gentile (Trophimus from Ephesus), they assumed he had brought Gentiles past the wall of the Temple.

So many arguments can be traced back to misunderstandings. These unnamed Jews had written a first draft in their heads about what Paul had done, and then came to believe their own narrative. They spread lies based on their false assumptions that led to riots, arrest, and all sorts of confusion.

What happened then still happens today: People often make assumptions about other people. We think someone looked at us judgmentally when maybe they didn't even see us. We think our friend's social media post was about us when it had nothing to do with us. We think someone purposely excluded us when in reality it was a small-group girls' gathering. Paul knew firsthand the chaos misunderstandings can cause, but he obeyed God's voice even when others cautioned him and tried to clear up a misunderstanding about his beliefs with action.

Daily Wrap-Up

What is one way you noticed God at work in Acts 21?

How did the believers respond?

God led Paul on a path that he knew ahead of time would be difficult. Paul knew what it meant to come up against misunderstandings and stay true to His convictions. We learn from Paul to obey the Lord even when others advise us to take an easier route. We also notice that the believers who warned him not to go to Jerusalem ultimately wanted the Lord's will rather than their own. Paul tried to sort out misunderstandings but was prepared for people to make wrong assumptions about him.

Today we focused on this truth: *we can follow God's leading in our lives without expecting everyone around us to understand our plans, methods, or motives.*

How would you summarize your personal takeaway from today's lesson?

When people make assumptions about us, it can be hurtful. One of our deepest longings is to be understood. We can rest in the truth that even if our closest friends can't see our side of things, Jesus understands. He knew what it was like to be rejected and still obey the Father's will. We take comfort in His example and learn to follow God even when those we love don't understand our choices.

Talk with God

Lord, help Your voice to be loudest in my life. When others don't understand what You've called me to do, give me holy boldness. Help me to love those who misunderstand me. Show me how I can contribute to greater understanding rather than division. Prepare me for the path You have ahead of me. I long to obey You rather than try to please the advice-givers around me. Give me discernment through Your Holy Spirit not to write my own silly first drafts about situations, but to see things clearly. Amen.

Memory Verse Exercise

Read the Memory Verse on page 140 several times, and then fill in the blanks below as you recite it:

But my _____ is worth _____ to me unless I use it for _____ the work assigned me by the Lord _____— the work of _____ _____ the _____ News about the wonderful _____ of God.

(Acts 20:24)

Day 3: Simplifying the Mission

Karen told me about her awakening to God and how much she wanted to share it with those she loved. She said, "I grew up in a 'good, church-going' home…not a born-again, spirit-filled family. I came to know the Lord as my Savior at twenty-one years old. I prayed for and talked to my parents and my two older brothers about Jesus through the years. I wouldn't say that I gave up, but my hope did wane over the years.

"My dad had a stroke and died five weeks later. However, he was aware of things and was able to respond to the call of Christ. My Mom, at eighty-three years old, slowly lost her will to live and acknowledged her need for a personal Savior in her last days. One of my brothers spoke of the hope of heaven because of the sacrifice of Jesus and accepted His forgiveness weeks before he died of cancer. My oldest brother never believed in God and didn't have any regard for God until he found out that he had terminal cancer and only months to live. He was a broken, hopeless, and scared man. God in His grace and mercy softened my brother's heart just a couple of weeks before he died, and my brother accepted Jesus as his Savior. God took my brother from death to life!

"It is through these life-changing and heart-wrenching experiences that God awakened my heart to His power. When someone you know is dying and they don't know Jesus…honestly nothing else matters. It was as if I couldn't help myself. I had to speak of Jesus and tell them once again about the eternal life-giving sacrifice of a loving Savior. There were days that I didn't know what I was going to say to them, but I think that's just where Jesus wanted me. It wasn't about me, and it wasn't because of my words. It was all about Him."

Karen didn't give up sharing her hope in Jesus with her family. She shared what Jesus had done in her life with intentionality and persistence. The apostle Paul kept telling his own personal story of transformation as well.

Read Acts 22:1-23 and map out Paul's testimony below.

Before Paul received Christ, he lived and thought this way (vv. 3-5):

How Paul received Christ (vv. 6-16):

After Paul received Christ, these changes took place (vv. 17-23):

Big Idea

Awakening to God's mission often happens as we simply share our personal story of faith in Jesus.

Extra Insights

Paul's life was radically transformed. He recalls with great clarity his salvation experience that happened twenty-five years prior.[15] I came to believe the gospel message when I was nine years old so my before-and-after story doesn't always feel very powerful to me. Yet I know that salvation should be more of a present reality than a past experience. Even if our stories don't seem as dynamic as Paul's, we want to be able to communicate the basics of our personal spiritual awakenings. We are going to review our own stories of coming to faith in a moment, but before we do that, let's take a moment to consider what God is doing now in our lives.

Write below a few notes about how you have seen God at work recently in your life:

Hopefully He has been encouraging, comforting, providing, showing Himself through the lives of other believers, and giving you hope even in your present trials. The apostle Peter challenged the recipients of his letter with these words: "And if someone asks about your hope as a believer, always be ready to explain it" (1 Peter 3:15b).

One of the most effective tools you have for sharing your faith is the story of how Jesus Christ gave you eternal life. When Paul stood before the crowd of Jews in Acts 22, he spoke simply, logically, and clearly about his life before salvation, how he met Christ, and what his life was like after conversion. Paul's testimony takes three or four minutes to read aloud in a conversational manner.

Let's answer the same questions we filled out for Paul. The purpose is to help those who consider themselves Christians recall the details of how we came to Christ.

Before I received Christ, I lived and thought this way:

How I received Christ:

After I received Christ, these changes took place:

We likely won't be telling our story in front of an angry mob, but, like Karen, we will want to be ready to share the words in the hospital room of a loved one or across the table from a friend at a coffee shop. We have the hope of the world in Jesus Christ. So many are sleepwalking through life without even realizing they need a spiritual awakening.

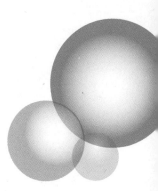

God is the One who wakes people from death to life spiritually, but He chooses to use us as His instruments. We want to be prepared to share the hope that we have in Christ. I've met people who have said they've just always been Christians. Being a Christian today can be associated with the religion or culture of our birth or our church upbringing. However, at some point, each one of us had to make a decision to believe that Jesus is *our* Savior.

If you struggled with knowing the details of your conversion, it doesn't mean you haven't made the journey. It can be like crossing a state line. I may not have realized the exact moment I left Ohio and crossed into Indiana, but I know that once I had been there, and now I am here. Some believers can't articulate the moment it happened, but they know that once they were lost in sin, but now they believe in Jesus.

The more articulately we know our own stories, the more ready we will be when opportunities to share about Jesus arise. We aren't responsible for the outcomes, but we want to be available to be used by God to share His message as a part of His mission that all men would be saved (1 Timothy 2:4).

It can be challenging for us when our stories don't end like Karen's did. We may have prayed for years and told those we love about Jesus, but they continue to reject the message. At times, I know I have felt like I must not have shared it correctly or that I've messed it up by not doing it right. It's important to remember that people who choose not to believe aren't rejecting you personally. Even when Paul shared his convincing evidence that Jesus is alive, it didn't always result in people coming to faith in Christ.

Read Acts 22:24-30 and label the following statements *T* for True or *F* for False:

_____The commander ordered Paul lashed with whips to make him confess his crime. (v. 24)

_____Paul asked if it was legal for them to whip a Greek citizen. (v. 25)

_____The soldiers quickly withdrew when they heard about his citizenship. (v. 29)

_____The next day, the commander ordered the Christian high council into session to find out what all the trouble was about. (v. 30)

Extra Insights

It amazes me that Paul knew in advance that he would face this kind of adversity in Jerusalem. He knew imprisonment and suffering awaited him, but he still went and told his story. He was ready to share about Christ whether it meant people would embrace the message or oppose it.

His example challenges me to remember my own story of spiritual awakening and be prepared to share the simple truth that I was a sinner separated from God until I recognized my need for God. At nine years of age, I knew that I needed something to fill the ache in my soul. I believed with childlike faith that Christ died for my sin and that God raised Him from the dead. When I believed in my heart and confessed with my mouth, I became a follower of Christ (Romans 10:9).

The road since then certainly hasn't been one of perfection, but it has included growing faith. I hope revisiting your salvation story today brought you back to the simplicity of the gospel message. God loves you. Sin separates people from God. Christ died so that we might know God. He fills us with His Spirit and commissions us to tell others about His great love.

If you want to believe in Christ but aren't sure if you are a Christian, turn to page 205 for "The Roman Road," a simple gospel explanation with Scriptures that clarify the gospel message.

Daily Wrap-Up

What is one way you noticed God at work in Acts 22?

How did the believers respond?

Paul boldly shared His story of meeting Jesus personally. When he told the Jews in Jerusalem that their God sent him to the Gentiles, they turned against him. He knew they wouldn't like that truth, but he told them what they needed to hear rather than what they wanted to hear. He kept his message centered on Christ. We can learn from Paul to be prepared to share what God has done in our lives even when we know others won't accept it.

Today we focused on this truth: *awakening to God's mission often happens as we simply share our personal story of faith in Jesus.*

How would you summarize your personal takeaway from today's lesson?

Karen kept praying and looking for opportunities to share Christ with those she loved. We will never argue anyone into the kingdom, but we do want to let others know what God has done in our lives. By preparing our stories, we don't want to memorize rote facts but instead get comfortable with the details so we can share them organically as God's Spirit leads us.

Talk with God

Lord, give me the right words to tell other people how good You have been to me. Sometimes I feel like I trip over my words or don't want others to feel like I'm judging them. Awaken me to see how I can talk about You just as I would talk about my family or friends whom I love. Holy Spirit, take over and show me opportunities to talk about Jesus in my everyday life. Amen.

Memory Verse Exercise

Read the Memory Verse on page 140 several times, and then fill in the blanks below as you recite it:

But my _____ is worth _____ to me _____ I use
it for _____ the work _____ me by the Lord
_____—the work of _____ _____ the _____
News _____ the wonderful _____ of God.

(**Acts 20:24**)

Day 4: Encouragement in Mission

I remember being frustrated with myself for taking it so hard. Watching my daughter deal with her diagnosis of alopecia included mourning the loss of her hair. I tried to be strong, encouraging, and supportive of my girl as we investigated wigs and eyebrow tattoos but in private, I often found myself crying and discouraged.

I told my mentor that I wished I had more faith in God. She told me that lamenting life's hardships didn't equate with a lack of faith. We are all working out our faith (Philippians 2:12). We can trust God while at the same time accept our human reactions. Sometimes it feels like we have to separate being a Christian from being a human. Today we will see that we can be both.

Scripture Focus

Acts 23

Big Idea

We can have human reactions to life's challenges while also awakening to supernatural possibilities.

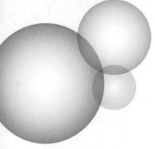

Extra Insights

More than a decade after Paul's trial, the high priest Ananias was hunted down and killed by Jewish guerrillas who found him hiding in an aqueduct near Herod's palace.[22]

The Jewish Sanhedrin "was composed of seventy...of the leading Jewish teachers, with the high priest presiding. It was their responsibility to interpret and apply the sacred Jewish law to the affairs of the nation, and to try those who violated that law."[25]

Paul certainly understood that he couldn't control all that was happening to him. Three principles from Acts 23 help us awaken to supernatural possibilities in our own lives today:

- Humans have human reactions.
- God's promises and presence give us power.
- We can expect God to work in unexpected places.

Read Acts 23:1-10 and note below any human reactions Paul displayed:

When slapped, Paul reacted by saying, "God will slap you, you corrupt hypocrite!" (Acts 23:3). While we know that Jesus didn't retaliate and made no threats when he was insulted (1 Peter 2:23), we see Paul's humanity on display. The Roman commander had been charged with keeping the peace in Jerusalem and had ordered a special session of the Jewish Sanhedrin to understand the cause of the riot. Paul had already been beaten by the crowd, chained, and barely escaped a severe beating at the hands of Roman soldiers. He addressed the council as brothers and immediately got slapped by the order of the high priest.

Ananias was known for his liberal use of brutal violence. His reputation was that of being pro-Roman and using his spiritual position to obtain money and power through scheming and bribery.[21]

Paul apologized for his comment once he was told the high priest had ordered the slap. It seemed odd that Paul wouldn't have recognized the high priest. Some have suggested that Paul never fully regained clear vision after his encounter on the road to Damascus because he often had others write his letters for him and signed them while mentioning his own large letters. Using large letters might have indicated a problem with his eyes. Another possibility includes Ananias not wearing his priestly robes because of the last-minute nature of the meeting.[23] Several other scholars suggested that Paul spoke ironically, proposing that no high priest would stoop so low as to have a man slapped.[24] Whether he couldn't see the high priest clearly or employed sarcasm, Paul quoted the Scriptures regarding not speaking evil of rulers (Exodus 22:28) in his apology. He respected the office of the high priest rather than the man who held the position.

We are made of the same stuff as Paul. We may not have been hit in the mouth, but we've been hit with a difficult relationship, an unexpected financial expense, a difficult health diagnosis, or some other circumstance that has felt like a slap in the face.

Can you think of a time when you have lashed out in frustration? If so, record the circumstances below:

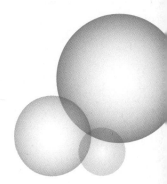

Humans have human reactions.

We don't want to beat ourselves up for being human. Even Jesus got angry, but he didn't sin in the midst of it (Mark 3:5). We learn from Paul that in spite of strong emotions, we can recognize when we are wrong, offer needed apologies, and not wallow in mistakes.

Paul pivoted from sorry to striking. He went on the offensive in the conversation by reading the room and dividing the Pharisees against the Sadducees. He redirected the conversation with a controversial topic like the Resurrection.

We often camp too long over what we wish we would or would not have said or done. We overthink perceived mistakes or omissions. From Paul we glimpse a man who didn't waste time in shame over his last mistake or human reaction. Instead, we can confess, seek God, and press on.

If you have been beating yourself up over a mistake or human reaction lately, below write a short prayer of confession and thanksgiving for God's grace, and ask God to help you seek out the next right step.

Confession:

Thanksgiving:

Next right step:

God's promises and presence give us power.

Not only can we reach out to God in the midst of our human realities, but often He reaches out to us.

Read Acts 23:11 and summarize this verse in your own words:

Paul was threatened with death but felt the urgency of the mission. The Lord graciously let him know that he would preach in Rome, giving Paul hope in the present. Though you may not have received a vision in the night like Paul, the Lord is standing near you right now saying, "Take courage." He is here. He has given us so many promises assuring us that He will never leave or forsake us (Deuteronomy 31:6; Hebrews 13:5).

Take a moment right now and envision the Lord standing right beside you. In whatever human realities you are facing, you are not alone. Meditate on His presence and list below one of the promises in the Bible that encourages you. (If nothing comes to mind, check out Psalm 23 and list one of the promises in that chapter below.)

Humans tend to have human reactions, but God's presence and promises bring us hope in the present. Now, let's uncover a final principle from Acts 23.

Read verses 12-35 and underline the people or groups of people in each statement. (I did the first one for you.)

- A <u>group of Jews</u> made an oath not to eat or drink until Paul was dead (12-13).
- These forty men told the leading priests and elders about their plan and asked them to have Paul brought back to the council so they could kill him on the way (14-15).
- Paul's nephew heard of the plan and told Paul and the Roman commander (16-22).
- The Roman commander organized almost four hundred Roman soldiers to protect Paul at different points on a journey to Caesarea where he would be placed in the custody of Governor Felix (23-35).

Did anything about these encounters strike you as surprising or unexpected? If so, write your thoughts below:

Here are a few of the ways I found the unexpected in these verses:

- It was surprising that forty men felt strongly enough to go without food or drink in order to see Paul dead. That feels overreactive as I think about their frustrations with him.
- In no other place in Scripture do we learn anything about Paul's extended family. Yet here we find he had a sister and a nephew. This mention of Paul's family was something I didn't see coming at this juncture in the story.
- The Roman army that crucified Christ and oppressed Christians was the force the Lord used to save Paul's life. I can't imagine that Paul or anyone else could have anticipated God's instruments of protection would be the Roman garrison!

Here is our final principle today:

Expect God to work in unexpected places.

What his own people sought for evil in Paul's life, God used for good. The Lord chose the Roman army for security and speed to get Paul to his next stop on God's divine platform so that he could share his testimony in new places with new audiences.

As you think about Paul's encounter, where have you seen God at work in unexpected places in your life?

As difficult as the human realities of my daughter's alopecia have been, over the course of almost a decade since her diagnosis, I have seen God at work. I am still learning to lament when my children are sad but not ride the roller coaster of their good or bad circumstances. I've also seen God turn my daughter's trial into her greatest triumph as she learned compassion and dependence on God in tangible ways through her situation.

I can imagine that you may have learned patience in difficult seasons or seen the Lord use unexpected resources to help you. As we continue to awaken our souls to God through our study in the book of Acts, we can expect the unexpected as we tune into God's plans rather than ours.

Daily Wrap-Up

What is one way you noticed God at work in Acts 23?

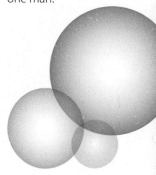

Extra Insight

The Roman protection afforded to Paul totaled 470 men, which "amounted to nearly half the Jerusalem garrison." This would have been a significant show of force for one man.[26]

How did the believers respond?

God allowed Paul to endure a slap in the face and unjust accusations. God also encouraged Paul very personally, giving him assurances of his ending up in Rome (Acts 23:11). In the midst of these human realities, the Lord enabled a nephew to overhear a plot and an ungodly organization to provide protection. Paul responded by embracing his humanity and owning his mistakes, but he also chose to believe God's promises rather than human circumstances.

Today we focused on this truth: *we can have human reactions to life's challenges while also awakening to supernatural possibilities.*

How would you summarize your personal takeaway from today's lesson?

I'm continuing to grow in not shaming myself for human reactions. When we accept our position of human weakness, we can lean into God's strength with greater intentionality. Paul learned to trust God in the midst of human realities, and we can too! Just as these principles were true for Paul, they are true for us:

- Humans have human reactions.
- God's promises and presence give us power.
- We can expect God to work in unexpected places.

So often we have limited control of what happens to us or those we love. But as we press into God, we can see ourselves not as victims of circumstance but on a journey to share the gospel with others.

Talk with God

Lord, I often struggle to make sense of how my life is contributing to Your mission. It would make more sense for me not to have so many trials and relationship struggles. Yet I believe that You want to work in ways I least expect. Help me to hold on to Your promises and presence when things look grim in my world. I want to take courage in You more than anything else. Thank You for Paul's example in Acts that awakens me to Your mission. Help me to trust You today. Amen.

Memory Verse Exercise

Read the Memory Verse on page 140 several times, and then fill in the blanks on the following page as you recite it:

_____ my _____ is worth _____ to me _____
I use it for _____ the _____ _____
me ____ _____ Lord _____—the _____ of
_____ _____ the _____ News _____ the
_____ _____ of God.

(Acts 20:24)

Day 5: Pressing Pause on the Mission

Two years. That was how long I struggled to get pregnant after a miscarriage in my nineteenth week of pregnancy. My husband and I were so grateful to have our bright-eyed two-year-old boy, but we grieved the loss of the baby we had expected.

I was amazed at how deeply I could miss someone I had never met. As soon as my body recovered, I really wanted to get pregnant again. I didn't anticipate two years of disappointed hopes month after month. Writing the words *two years* doesn't seem to capture the length of time I spent waiting and wondering what the future might hold.

Have you ever waited for something for more than a year? If so, describe below what you were hoping for and what you remember about the uncertainty of that season:

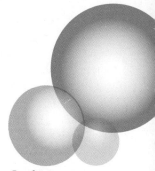

Scripture Focus

Acts 24

Big Idea

We can trust God with one opportunity at a time even when it feels like circumstances seem to press pause on our ability to move forward in serving God.

Today in Acts, we will find that Paul spent a season in limbo that lasted two years. My eyes sweep over that time frame without taking in the magnitude of:

- 730 days
- 17,520 hours
- 1,501,200 minutes
- 63,072,000 seconds

Typically, we have broken up our reading into segments, but today I would like us to read Acts 24 in its entirety.

Extra Insights

Drusilla was Felix's third wife who had been married previously to the ruler of a small kingdom in Syria at fifteen years old as arranged by her brother Agrippa II. She left this king for Felix and was about twenty years old when Paul arrived on the scene.[27]

Drusilla's family had a lot of history with Christianity. Her "great-grandfather tried to kill Jesus in Bethlehem (Matt. 2); her great-uncle killed John the Baptist and mocked Jesus (Luke 23:6-12); and Acts 12:1-2 tells of her father killing the apostle James."[28]

Summarize in your own words the following passages.

The charges brought by the lawyer Tertullus (vv. 2-6):

Paul's defense against the charges:

The timing (v. 11):

The lack of evidence (vv. 12-13):

His beliefs (vv. 14-16):

What actually happened in the Temple (vv. 17-21):

The charges brought against Paul included a personal, political, and a religious charge. He was labeled a troublemaker or plague (Acts 24:5a), charged with stirring up riots (Acts 24:5b), and accused of trying to desecrate the Temple (Acts 24:6). However, he defended himself boldly with truth.

Let's not forget that Paul had just completed his third missionary journey when he came to Jerusalem. Before we read the rest of the chapter, let's review the ground he has covered in the previous three years.

In these cities, he preached and welcomed new believers and encouraged seasoned Christians alike. He performed miracles and shared his personal story of faith. To say he had a productive season would be an understatement.

As you read the following chart summarizing only a few of the events along the journey, circle the city on the map that corresponds and write the key word from the chart near that city (I did the first one for you):

Verses	Event	People involved	City	Key Word
Acts 19:11	Paul preached at the hall of Tyrannus and performed unusual miracles.	Jews and Greeks	Ephesus	Miracles
Acts 20:2-4	Paul encouraged the believers in all the towns he passed through.	Sopater, Aristarchus, Secundus, Gaius, Timothy, Tychicus, and Trophimus were all traveling companions	Macedonia	Encourage

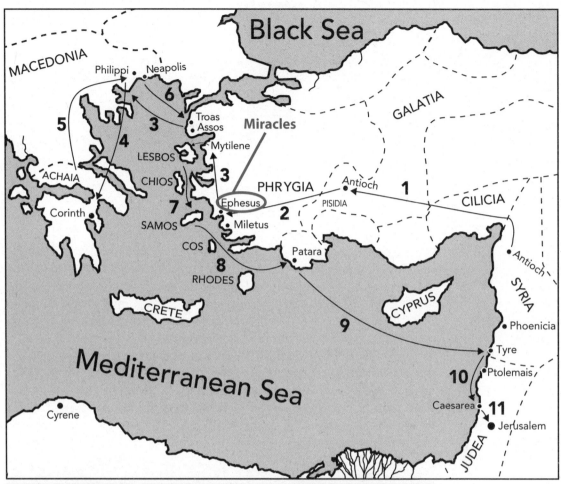

Verses	Event	People involved	City	Key Word
Acts 20:9-10	A boy fell out a window while Paul was preaching.	Eutychus	Troas	Preach
Acts 20:36-38	Paul prayed, cried, and said goodbye to the elders he had served alongside for years.	Ephesian Elders	Miletus	Goodbyes
Acts 21:10-14	Agabus prophesied suffering ahead for Paul, and the local believers begged him not to go to Jerusalem.	Agabus, Philip and his prophetic daughters, local believers	Caesarea	Prophecy
Acts 22:3-21	After being arrested, Paul shared his personal testimony with a crowd in Jerusalem.	Jewish leaders, Roman commander, Jewish crowd	Jerusalem	Testimony

While these circumstances weren't always easy, Paul certainly couldn't have claimed boredom!

As you reflect on your life, can you remember a time when it felt like you were really going places and doing things—whether in your career, family life, or ministry? If so, write about what you accomplished during that time below.

Extra Insight

"Paul was kept in Herod's praetorium, the palace which had been built by Herod the Great and now served as the headquarters of the Roman administration."[29] This government headquarters near the sea likely had comfortable accommodations for high-profile prisoners.[30]

I remember one season when I oversaw a family ministries project at our church. The ministry team and participants seemed energized by this program, and many of my close friends were on the leadership team serving alongside. Just when I sensed this great momentum, God called my husband to a new ministry. When we faced challenges in the new ministry, I often looked back on the excitement of the other project with longing.

Paul went through changing ministry seasons as well. He knew suffering lay ahead in Jerusalem, but I don't know if he was prepared for the ambiguity he faced in Caesarea. Jesus had assured him in a vision that he would get to Rome (Acts 23:11), but I wonder if he grew frustrated during the two years when the mission seemed to stall. He could easily have focused on all the things he couldn't do or look for ways to be effective within his limitations.

Read again the following verses and make a note of what Paul was able to do during this restrictive season:

v. 23

vv. 24-25

v. 26

Paul had some access to his friends. He also got to share the gospel with Felix and Drusilla. Some have suggested that Luke was one of the friends visiting Paul during this season, compiling information that would inform the writing of his Gospel and the Book of Acts![31]

Our waiting seasons may not include jail time, but there are times when we can't do all that we would like to do because of:

- health limitations,
- caring for small children or aging parents,
- work obligations, or
- financial restrictions.

What other circumstances could you add to this list?

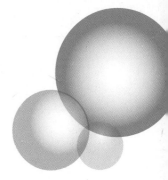

When God pushes the pause button in our lives, we can get frustrated. Like me, you might compare the current challenges with past productivity. Like Paul, you could learn to do what you can with what you have.

Whether you are in a slow season right now or not, what can you do to serve others and share God's message in your sphere of influence?

If you had trouble thinking of something, the women in my pilot group noted these activities that might give you a springboard as you ask God to awaken you to see the needs of others around you:

- praying;
- discipling teenagers or children through church ministries;
- making disciples at home with intentional parenting;
- leading/participating in Bible studies;
- volunteering with an organization that serves people in need;
- offering friendship to those who are lonely;
- spending time with senior citizens;
- going on mission trips or supporting others to go; or
- small acts of kindness like paying for someone's groceries, letting another person go first, taking a meal to a sick person.

Fulfilling God's Great Commission of making disciples can take on many different shapes according to our spiritual gifts and the needs around us.

Hearing the word *mission* can be overwhelming, as though it must be some sort of trip or grand ministry. Instead, it often looks more like baby steps as we see needs and seek to meet them. As we awaken to God, His Spirit guides our thoughts and decisions as we look to do the next right things in loving the people around us.

Sometimes we may feel purposeful and productive in sharing Christ's love. Other times, we sense a lull with circumstances that limit us. Instead of measuring the results of our efforts, we can focus on listening to the Holy Spirit. He may direct us to activities like resting, waiting, and praying and other times it might look more like traveling, teaching, or encouraging. Awakening to God means allowing Him to decide whether to press go or pause as we discover our unique callings to serve.

Daily Wrap-Up

What is one way you noticed God at work in Acts 24?

How did the believers respond?

Two years of confinement likely would not have been Paul's first choice of assignment if he could have picked. It can be difficult to reconcile the urgency of sharing God's message with the limitations we often find in our circumstances. From Acts 24, I've been challenged to focus on what I can do rather than what I can't.

Today we focused on this truth: *we can trust God with one opportunity at a time even when it feels like circumstances seem to press pause on our ability to move forward in serving God.*

How would you summarize your personal takeaway from today's lesson?

Two years seemed so long when I was waiting to get pregnant. I imagine that Paul clung in faith to the promise that eventually he would get to Rome to share the gospel, but the two years of waiting had to have been challenging for him. Times of uncertainty and limitation can be difficult for us as well. As we awaken to God's Spirit, we can trust Him to lead us in both productive and restrictive seasons of ministry.

Talk with God

Lord, I don't like waiting. I also struggle when situations seem useless or unproductive. There are so many people that need to know Your love. Yet so many times it feels like I'm stuck in limiting situations. Help me to trust Your promises when I feel restricted and restless. Awaken me to your Holy Spirit to learn to wait well. Give me eyes to see opportunities I may have missed to serve You and love those around me in practical ways. Amen.

Memory Verse Exercise

Read the Memory Verse on page 140 several times, and then fill in the blanks below as you recite it:

_____ ____ _____ *is worth* _____ *to me* _____

I _____ *it for* _____ *the* _____ _____

me ____ _____ _____ _____—*the* _____ *of*

_____ _____ *the* _____ _____ _____

the _____ _____ *of* _____.

(Acts 20:24)

Weekly Wrap-Up

Review the Big Idea for each day, and then write any personal application that comes to mind.

Day 1: A Mission Worth the Sacrifices

Big Idea: sharing the good news can present challenges in our lives, but remembering the eternal impact of the mission realigns our perspective.

Personal Application:_____

_____

Day 2: Misunderstanding and the Mission

Big Idea: we can follow God's leading in our lives without expecting everyone around us to understand our plans, methods, or motives.

Personal Application:_____

_____

Day 3: Simplifying the Mission

Big Idea: awakening to God's mission often happens as we simply share our personal story of faith in Jesus.

Personal Application:_____

_____

Day 4: Encouragement in Mission

Big Idea: we can have human reactions to life's challenges while also awakening to supernatural possibilities.

Personal Application:_____

_____

Day 5: Pressing Pause on the Mission

Big Idea: we can trust God with one opportunity at a time even when it feels like circumstances seem to press pause on our ability to move forward in serving God.

Personal Application:_____

_____

Video Viewer Guide: Week 5

Acts 20:18-27

Two extremes about mission:

Mission can be _____.

Mission can be _____.

Micah 6:8

We find our purpose in _____.

Action step: What is one small change you can make in your thinking, your attitude, or your actions that would help you remember that your aim is faithfulness?

We find our power through _____.

In the Bible, we see _____ as a virtue 200 times.

Week 6

Awakening to God's Direction

Acts 25–28

Memory Verse

"'And I will rescue you from both your own people and the Gentiles. Yes, I am sending you to the Gentiles to open their eyes, so they may turn from darkness to light and from the power of Satan to God. Then they will receive forgiveness for their sins and be given a place among God's people, who are set apart by faith in me.'"

(Acts 26:17-18)

Day 1: Direction in Decisions

When our children were in grade school, my husband and I wanted to teach them not to argue back when we made a parental decision. However, we also learned that children need to learn a respectful way to make an appeal.

In the hustle and bustle of church activities, sport practices, and homework, sometimes we didn't possess every piece of information before making a judgment. If we told the kids they couldn't have friends over because they needed to do chores, they needed to listen without interrupting. Then they could ask to make an appeal. They might want us to know that they had already completed their chores, and their friends were already waiting for them outside.

Other times they would ask to make an appeal and didn't add any relevant information. They quickly learned that if they wanted us to take appeals seriously, they should use them sparingly and when they had logical arguments.

The appeal process continues long past childhood as we recognize that decisions often need to be revisited in light of new information. Employers, family members, and governing authorities provide directives that impact our lives. Sometimes we agree with their decisions, and other times we want to make an appeal.

In the final chapters of Acts, we find Paul appealing a bad decision. Felix had left Paul in prison, delaying his case for two years. When a new governor/proconsul took Felix's place, Paul must have had some hope that his waiting season might soon be over. He knew the charges against him were flimsy at best.

Read Acts 25:1-12 and write in the chart below a few of the decisions you observe by the people below:

Person/People	Verses	Decisions made
Festus	4-5, 9, 12	
Jewish leaders	2-3, 7	
Paul	8, 10-11	

Big Idea

While it may seem like other people control our lives, we can seek God in our decisions knowing that He has ultimate authority.

Extra Insight

Acts 25 fulfills the Lord's promise that Paul would be a witness before "Gentiles and . . . kings" (Acts 9:15).

Festus wanted to establish good relations with the Jewish leaders, but he listened to his advisors and thus allowed Paul's appeal to Caesar to stand. The Jewish leaders operated in fear with lies and a murderous plot. The Lord had told Paul that he would get to Rome so he didn't need to fear (Acts 23:11). He stood his ground and ultimately appealed to a higher court, knowing he wouldn't find justice in the Jewish council.

Paul navigated the control of other people while at the same time controlling himself. He ultimately knew that God's will would prevail. While it may seem like other people control our lives, we can seek God in our decisions, knowing He has ultimate control over the direction of our lives.

As you consider your life right now, is there an area where other people's decisions are affecting you? (If so, write about it briefly below.)

If you are currently feeling the weight of others' choices, what are some decisions that you face as you respond to those choices? (Be sure to consider attitudes as well as actions.)

Ultimately, God is in control of our futures. We can rest in the truth that His purposes will prevail. Like Paul we can remain thoughtful and clearheaded as we look to the Lord for direction. Sometimes He may call us to accept our circumstances; other times, we might feel prompted to make an appeal. After Paul made his decision to appeal to Caesar, we get some insight into Festus's concerns.

Read Acts 25:13-22 and write below what surprised Festus regarding the charges brought against Paul, according to verses 18-19:

I'm not sure exactly what Festus expected, but it wasn't a conversation about Jesus. Paul's decision to be levelheaded gave him an opportunity to speak about Christ.

What are some common reactions when a person is falsely accused?

I know I've lashed back, showed anger, or felt overcome by fear, making it difficult to articulate my thoughts and feelings. Emotions are important. When we've been mistreated, emotions can run high. Yet if I look back at my emotional decisions, I wouldn't say they were usually my best ones. I doubt that Paul enjoyed seeing his accusers again after so much time had passed, but he didn't allow their presence to trigger a fear-based response. He stood up for himself and spoke boldly about Jesus while maintaining his composure.

As you reflect on these verses, what can you learn from Festus, Paul, and the Jewish leaders regarding decision-making:

Positive examples—(what to do)

Negative examples—(what not to do)

Extra Insight

The emperor whom Paul appealed to was Nero. While he became known for his cruelty to Christians after the fire that burned Rome in AD 64, this incident occurred during the earlier years of his reign when he was considered more stable and reasonable.[1]

Paul stated his case authoritatively and made an appeal when necessary. Festus sought counsel and tried to understand the issues. The Jewish leaders provided negative examples in their decisions to falsely accuse, tell lies, and plot a murder rather than seek justice.

They wanted to eliminate the competition of a new religion, and they thought getting rid of Paul was the answer. They should have heeded Gamaliel's warning that they might find themselves fighting against God Himself if they weren't careful (Acts 5:39). Their decisions were driven by jealousy and fear.

Paul recognized that people like Felix and Festus made decisions that affected him, but he knew that none of their choices could thwart God's plan in his life. Let's bring that principle a little closer to home.

As you think about circumstances outside of your control, how could awakening to God's ultimate authority in the direction of your life change your mindset?

Extra Insight

Bernice was the sister of both Drusilla (Felix's wife) and Agrippa II. By the age of twenty-one, she had been widowed twice and came to live with her brother. Rumors of incest swept the kingdom so she was married again but left the marriage and engaged in a "well-known love affair" with Titus, the son of Vespasian, who would later become the emperor of Rome.[2]

With the help of a wise counselor during a turbulent time in my life, I recognized that I had struggled with making fear-based parenting decisions. I've overly monitored my child and freaked out at times when I didn't know her exact location. Because of past occurrences, my mind quickly played out worst-case scenarios, which led me to strong emotions. These fear-based, controlling behaviors led to a greater wedge in my relationship with my child. My intent was protection, but my decisions left wounds in their wake. I've come to realize that there is a difference between intent and impact. I didn't intend harm, but my decisions had a harmful impact on our relationship. I am now working to trust God (and my child) so that I can respond rather than react while at the same time believing that ultimately the Lord is in control. Acts 25 reminds me to trust God's greater plan more than my fears.

Festus gives us one last principle to hold on to as we consider our decisions. Rather than rush to judgment, he took an investigative posture toward Paul's situation.

Read Acts 25:23-27 and describe what Festus was looking for, according to verses 26-27?

When a prisoner appealed to a higher court during this time in history, the file "required a cover letter summarizing the case's facts in a way that displayed some investigation. Sending a report along with the prisoner was a mandatory procedure." This rule likely motivated Festus's investigation.[3]

Festus wanted clarity in muddy circumstances. He didn't understand the Jews' charges or Paul's explanation. He asked his friend Agrippa to help him examine the situation more closely through listening.

As you consider any upcoming choices in the days and weeks ahead, how might listening to God and other people inform your decision?

When we take a humble posture that recognizes our need to listen and learn, we can grow in discernment. This will help us awaken to God's direction as we seek to know and understand the impact of our choices.

Today we learned that:

❑ others' decisions impact our lives,

❑ we have choices to make in response to those decisions, and

❑ ultimately God is in control of our future.

Put a check mark next to the truth above that most resonates with you today.

Daily Wrap-Up

What is one way you noticed God at work in Acts 25?

How did the believers respond?

Luke didn't write much about God in this chapter, yet we see Him at work. He made sure Paul was protected through the actions of Festus. Paul responded with an appeal to Caesar because He trusted God's assurances about going to Rome.

Paul believed God more than his own fear, so he responded to those who had influence over his life with boldness. We can learn from him not to cower under those who seem to have control in our lives and focus instead on making decisions that honor the Lord.

Today we focused on this truth: *while it may seem like other people control our lives, we can seek God in our decisions knowing that He has ultimate authority.*

How would you summarize your personal takeaway from today's lesson?

Decisions can be challenging, especially when we feel like others are controlling us. Like my children, we can appeal seemingly unjust decisions. Like Paul, we can trust God's direction for our lives so we don't make choices rooted in fear. Through postures of trust and listening, we can follow God's direction for our lives.

Talk with God

Lord, help me to remember that no one can thwart Your plan for me. Help me not to allow fear to bring out controlling behaviors in my life. I don't want to be like the Jewish leaders who hunted Paul. Instead, I want my trust in You to guide me into boldness and clarity. As I think about the choices facing me this week, I'm asking for Your direction. Awaken me to see You at work. Amen.

Memory Verse Exercise

Read the Memory Verse on page 170 several times, and then fill in the blanks below as you recite it:

" 'And I will _____ you from both your own people and the

_____. Yes, I am sending you to the Gentiles to open their

eyes, so they may turn from darkness to light and from the power of

_____ to God. Then they will receive _____

for their sins and be given a place among God's people, who are set

apart by faith in me.' "

(Acts 26:17-18)

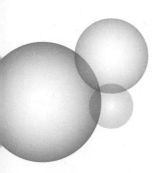

Day 2: Directed toward God

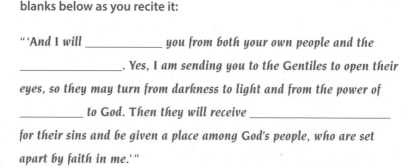

Scripture Focus

Acts 26

Big Idea

We can make the most of every opportunity to direct people toward God.

Canoeing without oars can be a frustrating experience. When someone desires to head upstream toward a destination, the person will find himself or herself drifting in the opposite direction without oars. While teaching teenagers over the years, I've often used a canoe metaphor to describe the life a Christ-follower. Difficult life circumstances and the current of culture can pull one's "life" canoe downstream—away from God. Sin, self-sufficiency, and counterfeit gods embedded into our music, media, and conversations can drag us down with subtle or overt messages. God provides many different oars to help us in our pursuit of a close relationship with Him. Two that I find vital in my own journey of movement toward the Lord are Bible study and prayer. These spiritual rhythms provide connection with God and realignment to truth.

What other practices help direct you toward God? How could these practices help you direct others toward God?

Perhaps you wrote things like resting, gathering with other believers, or taking a nature walk. The apostle Paul tried to make the most of every opportunity to direct others toward God. Today we'll read the third recording of his testimony in Acts. Rather than wonder why we are revisiting the same story again, let's read Acts 26 with great anticipation, knowing that God often repeats what He wants to emphasize.

Read Acts 26:1-23 and choose the best answer for the statements:

1. King Agrippa told Paul he could speak in (v. 1):

   A. his own language, or

   B. his own defense.

2. Paul asked Agrippa to listen patiently and started his defense using (v. 1):

   A. a hand gesture, or

   B. a verbal attack on his accusers.

3. Paul felt fortunate that Agrippa could hear his defense because he was an expert on (v. 3):

   A. Gentile customs and controversies, or

   B. Jewish customs and controversies.

4. Paul stated that he was on trial for (v. 6):

   A. his hope in the fulfillment of God's promises regarding a Messiah, or

   B. his Jewish training as a Pharisee.

While Paul's testimony is included three times in Acts, this account revealed new details regarding the brightness of the light, the impact on both Paul *and* his companions, the fact that they all fell to the ground, and the voice from heaven speaking in Aramaic. These added facts don't contradict the other accounts of Paul's testimony but bring greater clarity to the encounter.[4]

"The word *minister* in Acts 26:16 means 'an under-rower' and refers to a lowly servant on a galley ship. Paul had been accustomed to being an honored leader, but after his conversion he became a subordinate worker, and Jesus Christ became his Master."[5] (Your translation may have translated the Greek word as *servant* rather than *minister* here.)

5. Paul said he previously opposed the name of Jesus by (vv. 9-11):

   A. disregarding it; or

   B. imprisoning, punishing, and chasing down Christians.

6. Paul said that on the road to Damascus he had a conversation with (vv. 14-18):

   A. Jesus, or

   B. an unidentified voice.

7. To obey that vision, Paul said he (vv. 19-20):

   A. preached that all must repent of their sins and turn to God in Damascus, Jerusalem, all Judea, and to the Gentiles; or

   B. preached that the Messiah was only for the Jews.

8. Paul said his teaching was in line with the prophets believing that the (v. 23):

   A. messiah would conquer and free them from Roman rule, or

   B. messiah would suffer and rise from the dead.

As you reflect on Paul's defense, what are some ways that Paul directed his listeners toward God?

Paul certainly could have made these issues the focus of his defense:

- being stuck in prison for two years under Felix,
- his rights as a Roman citizen, or
- the injustice of the false charges brought against him.

Instead, Paul made the most of the opportunity to share his personal story of life transformation. The trajectory of his life completely changed, and he wanted to help others direct their lives toward the living God. He gave some background, shared his story, and explained the path that led to God.

Answers: 1. B, 2. A, 3. B, 4. A, 5. B, 6. A, 7. A, 8. B.

How would you summarize in a sentence how a person far from God can move toward God, according to Paul (Acts 26:20):

Maybe you said something like, "Repent of sin and turn toward God by believing that Jesus is the Messiah." Perhaps you said it another way. Paul's mission was to open spiritual eyes. Through his physical blinding, he found spiritual sight. He wanted everyone to awaken to the truth about Jesus.

Too many times I am focused on the injustices in my life and those around me. I defend myself and focus on the wrong that's been done to me. Paul likely worked through his emotions regarding his circumstances but chose to speak about God's work in his life.

Where might you need a change of focus in your life right now?

Rather than focus on what's been done to us, we can zero in on what God has done for us. As we think about directing other people toward God, we can remember that Paul prayed, knew his audience, and depended on the Lord for direction. He didn't shove truth down people's throats but instead sought to present it in a way that would help them see clearly.

For many years, I met weekly with a group of moms from my children's school to pray. The organizer of the group used the list of students and staff at the school and divided them up so that by the end of the year we had prayed for one another by name. Acts 26:18 was often used as a prayer prompt.

As you think of someone in your life who needs direction toward God, plug their name into this verse as you stop for a moment and pray for them:

I pray that _____'s eyes would be opened, "so they may turn from darkness to light and from the power of Satan to God. Then they will receive forgiveness for their sins and be given a place among God's people, who are set apart by faith."

(Acts 26:18)

Extra Insights

Paul used a well-known idiom to explain that the events he referenced were not done "in a corner" in Acts 26:26. The Christian movement was familiar to most people at that time.[6]

———————

After Festus and Agrippa heard Paul's testimony, they said he could have been let go if he hadn't appealed to Caesar. Culturally this was a matter of "honor and propriety." "It would dishonor both Festus and the emperor not to follow through."[7]

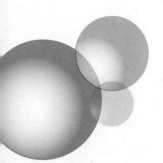

Now reflect and listen for any spiritual nudges toward practical ways you can show love toward this individual in the coming weeks. Write below any ideas that come to mind:

Praying, showing love, and speaking truth are steps we can take, but the responses to our efforts will likely vary. Throughout the course of this study, we've seen Peter, Paul, and many other disciples share the message of Christ. Sometimes people repented and believed. Other times they hurled rocks or chased the believers out of town. Let's finish the chapter to see how Festus and Agrippa responded to Paul's testimony.

Read Acts 26:24-32 and summarize the reactions of:

Festus (v. 24)

Agrippa (v. 28)

If Paul was measuring success by responses, he would have marked zero for two on conversions. Yet he wasn't called to control outcomes but to share the message (Matthew 28:19-20). In the same way, we can't force people to believe in God. Instead, we focus on directing them toward Him as best we can and leave the results in His hands. I often want to rush the process of someone knowing Jesus personally.

What did Paul say in Acts 26:29 about the direction he desired everyone to take, whether quickly or not?

Paul unashamedly spoke that he prayed and desired everyone in the room to become a Christian. We discover in this verse that Paul didn't appear privately before Festus, Agrippa, and Bernice. They had assembled a larger audience to hear Paul's defense, and Paul wanted all of them to move toward God.

Today we've talked a lot about directing other people toward the Lord. What is one practical way you can draw nearer to the Lord?

Maybe you will sit and think about eternal truths in light of temporal concerns. Perhaps you'll listen, pray, journal, sing, or call a friend. Paul clung to Jesus and invited others to move toward Him.

Daily Wrap-Up

What is one way you noticed God at work in Acts 26?

How did the believers respond?

While these verses don't specifically say that the Holy Spirit was leading Paul, he responded by making the focus of his defense the work of God rather than his personal injustices. We can learn from Paul to move toward God and direct others to do the same.

Today we focused on this truth: *we can make the most of every opportunity to direct people toward God.*

How would you summarize your personal takeaway from today's lesson?

Sometimes knowing which way to turn will be difficult. We should ask ourselves in each situation, "How can I move toward God in this?" When we experience His power and nearness, we might then ask a second question, "How can I direct others toward God?" Even when we find ourselves at a crossroads, we will find spiritual direction as we take steps toward God. The culture may be pulling us downstream, but God provides oars to help us in our journey to move closer to Him.

Talk with God

Lord, I often don't know what to do. Help me to lean toward You—especially when life feels confusing. Give me the spiritual rhythms I need to move upstream so the culture doesn't drag me far from You. Turn my thoughts from what's happened to me to what You have done for me through Christ. Use me Lord to direct others toward You. Awaken me to spiritual movement! Amen.

Memory Verse Exercise

Read the Memory Verse on page 170 several times, and then fill in the blanks below as you recite it:

And I will _____ you from _____ your own people and the _____. Yes, I am sending you to the Gentiles to _____ their _____, so they may turn from _____ to light and from the power of _____ to God. Then they will receive _____ for their _____ and be given a place among God's _____, who are set apart by _____ in me.

(Acts 26:17-18)

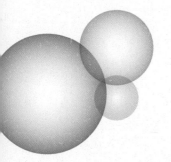

Day 3: Boldness in Dangerous Directions

Scripture Focus

Acts 27

Big Idea

God calls us to boldly trust His directions and encourage others even in the stormiest seasons of life.

Growing up in East Texas meant frequently hearing tornado sirens blaring, and our family huddling together in a safe place to wait out a storm. One particular time I was at my grandma's house, and my mom was perming my hair when the winds began to howl. She was in the middle of it when the storm got worse, and it was deemed necessary to head to the storm shelter buried underground on their forty acres. My attitude could have been described as anything but bold. I worried that if the storm didn't get us, my hair would be fried from the perm chemicals being left in too long. Thankfully the storm blew over, and we ran back to the house to take out the rollers and rinse the chemicals out before any permanent damage was done. (Unless you count that 1980s hairstyle my perm accomplished that I teased until it almost reached God Himself!)

Can you think of a time when some weather conditions outside caused you concern? If so, write about it below:

Today we'll find Paul heading straight into a storm.

Read Acts 27:1-12 and summarize below the bold directions Paul gave to the ship's officers (v. 10):

Paul may have been a prisoner, but he didn't hesitate to offer his insight. We've seen throughout the Book of Acts that being filled with the Holy Spirit often evidences itself in boldness in a believer's life. Paul's advice about staying at Fairhavens came from God, but he wasn't someone unfamiliar with storms and ships. "Paul had already experienced three shipwrecks (2 Cor. 11:25), so he was certainly speaking from experience."[8]

When Christians in Acts followed the leading of the Spirit, they didn't care as much about earthly consequences or people's opinions. Paul's advice wasn't arrogance but boldness to trust God more than logic or emotions. This boldness believed that God was in control of all their lives so they didn't need to fear the decisions of mere humans.

As you reflect on your journey of following Jesus, can you think of a time that the Holy Spirit gave you boldness? If so, write about it briefly below:

It's OK if nothing came to mind right away. Sometimes the quality of boldness can be hard to come by. Other times, it can be difficult to claim what you've done as being bold. But I've seen women around me boldly walk away from abuse with the Holy Spirit's help. Some have spoken about Christ in hostile environments. Others have boldly fought to overcome addictions. Seven times in Acts we find the Greek word for boldness associated with Paul. *Parrhesiazomai* means, "to use freedom in speaking, be free spoken . . . to speak freely . . . to grow confident, have boldness, show assurance, assume a bold bearing."[11]

Let's return to Paul's story for more examples of his confidence.

Read Acts 27:13-26 and make notes below of some of the challenges faced and the bold attitude displayed by Paul:

Challenges faced (vv. 14, 17, 18, 20):

Extra Insights

Luke and Aristarchus accompanied Paul on the journey to Rome. Commentators deduce that Luke might have come as Paul's personal doctor based on the "we" language used throughout the chapter. Colossians 4:10 and Philemon 24 document Aristarchus sending his greetings from Rome.[9]

"Because ships transported cargos and only incidentally carried passengers, they did not provide services. . . . Officers like Julius would requisition transport and food for their party." Most passengers would have brought their own food for the journey.[10]

Paul's attitude (vv. 21-26):

Can you picture the passengers on this ship? I can't imagine what it would be like for days on end with the sun and stars blotted out by a storm. It must have felt terrifying, like it would never end. We may not be going through a physical storm, but sometimes the difficulties in our lives leave us in dark places that we feel may never end.

As you consider your life right now, is there a situation where you could use a little more confidence? If so, write about it below:

I have often struggled with confidence over the course of my life. If I could go back and talk to myself as a teenager, a young married woman, a mom, an employee, and so on, one of the things I would want to say to my younger self would be to have more confidence. I fretted way too much over what *might* happen or what others *might* think.

But as I'm growing in faith, I see the power of fear and comparison losing their grip in my life. I'm praying that as we awaken to God's direction through His Holy Spirit, we would discover more boldness. Since I can't talk to my younger self, let me encourage you where you are right now. Be confident in where the Lord has you. He is working. He loves you. Be bold in Him!

Paul showed us that we don't have to cower when life gets stormy. He encouraged those around him to take courage because of the God to whom he belonged and served. I don't know if anyone believed this prisoner when he told them it would be all right, but moments of despair can become opportunities.

As we continually awaken to supernatural possibilities, the fears associated with our stormy seasons lose their power.

Write a short prayer below, asking the Lord to help you see any current challenges from His perspective:

In addition to prayer, many other practices like studying the Bible and talking with encouraging Christian friends can help us realign to faith over fear. Changing our questions can also shift our perspective. Instead of saying, "Why me?" we can ask, "What's next?" Paul definitely seemed to have a "What's next?" posture, even when he was imprisoned in a sinking ship.

Read Acts 27:27-44 and answer the following questions:

What were the sailors praying for? (v. 29)

This time when Paul gave the commanding officers and soldiers his opinion, how did they respond? (vv. 31-32)

What did all 276 passengers do because of Paul's advice? (v. 36)

What happened to destroy the ship? (v. 41)

Why did the commanding officer decide not to follow the soldiers' advice regarding the prisoners? (vv. 42-43)

How many passengers escaped safely to shore? (v. 44)

As you reflect on this incident, how might the passengers have been impacted by Paul's boldness?

Extra Insight

"The itinerary, weather conditions, and sailors' actions are correct down to minute details in most of 27:1–28:15."[13] So we know the Acts account provides accurate information that aligns with the schedules, winds, and sailing techniques in the first century in that region.

I wonder if some asked more questions about his God. Others may not have cared once they had made it to safety. What we do know is that allowing God's

Spirit to direct our lives often evidences itself in boldness. This doesn't mean we never experience fear or doubt. Luke didn't record Paul's every thought and feeling while on that ship. He likely had some human moments. However, we can work through our fears and doubts and trust God more than our human realities. When we do, the Lord might direct us to encourage others in their storms. Like Paul, we can say things like:

- Take courage (vv. 22, 25).
- Don't be afraid (v. 24).
- God is good (v. 24).
- I believe God (v. 25).

How can you bring encouragement to others in your life?

If nothing comes to mind right now, ask the Spirit to direct you and be sure to follow through on any ideas this week.

Life will have its rainy seasons, but just like the weather, we can trust God that our seasons will eventually change. We can place our trust in Him and anticipate our own seasons of "what's next" in our lives.

Daily Wrap-Up

What is one way you noticed God at work in Acts 27?

How did the believers respond?

God sent an angel to encourage Paul in a dangerous storm. His Holy Spirit empowered Paul with holy boldness to speak up whether his words were welcome or not. We don't want to be spiritual bullies, but we can speak up boldly as the Spirit leads us to bring God's encouragement to those walking through difficult days.

Today we focused on this truth: *God calls us to boldly trust His directions and encourage others even in the stormiest seasons of life.*

How would you summarize your personal takeaway from today's lesson?

I want to learn to ask "What's next?" instead of "Why me?" when the weather abruptly changes in my life. Storms and shipwrecks may not be literal for us, but we've likely encountered circumstances where we've felt threatened or scared. We don't have to hide and wait out the storms that come into our lives. We can boldly seek God and encourage others by reminding them of His love and concern.

Talk with God

Lord, I don't like hard circumstances. Sometimes I just wish life could be easier. Help me to move past my "why's" so I can ask "what's next?" So, Lord, what's next? Show me how I can boldly trust You with my tomorrows and encourage those around me to do the same. Holy Spirit, give me boldness to believe all that God has promised. Wake me up to supernatural possibilities today! Amen.

Memory Verse Exercise

Read the Memory Verse on page 170 several times, and then fill in the blanks below as you recite it:

_____ I will _____ you from _____ your own _____ and the _____. Yes, I am sending you to the Gentiles to _____ their _____, so they may _____ from _____ to _____ and from the power of _____ to God. Then they will _____ _____ for their _____ and be _____ a place among God's _____, who are _____ apart by _____ in me.

(Acts 26:17-18)

Day 4: Directed to Faithfulness

My first day of college left me a little syllabus-shocked. Each professor overviewed a schedule of assignments, reminding us that we were now in college and would not receive reminders for tests and papers. However, it wasn't an exam or ten-page paper that gnawed at my stomach as I trekked from the academic building to my dorm. My class titled "Personal Evangelism" required each student to share our faith with at least two people over the course of the

Scripture Focus

Acts 28

Big Idea

God calls us to faithfulness so that He can bring greater fruitfulness.

semester. We didn't have to convert anyone, we just had to personally share our testimony with two individuals.

I had just moved from suburban Texas to inner-city Chicago, and everyone at my school had a ministry major so I wracked my brain to think of who these two people might be. I went to my room and wrote my fears in a journal. In those moments I felt the Holy Spirit encourage me that He would help me. His Spirit would produce the fruit; I needed only to be faithful.

Too many times I have worried rather than believed two important truths that we'll be reminded of in the last chapter of Acts:

- God supplies the supernatural power we need for anything He directs us to do.
- Outcomes are in God's hands.

Read Acts 28:1-10 and choose from these key words to fill in the boxes above the line, putting the events in order on a story diagram: (I labeled two of them for you.)

Key words:

Adored—When Paul didn't die from the snakebite, he was deemed a god.
Supplied—Paul was showered with honors and given supplies for the next part of his journey.
Accused—When Paul was bitten by a snake, the islanders assumed he was a murderer who needed to be punished.
Prayer—When Paul prayed and laid hands on Publius's father, he was healed.
Healing—After the Lord used Paul to heal Publius's father, many other sick came to Paul and were healed.
Shipwrecked—After the shipwreck, the passengers were welcomed by the people of Malta, who built fires for them since it was cold and rainy.

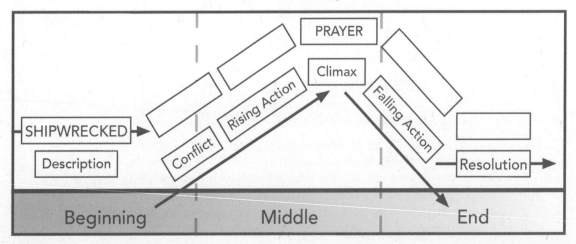

In Paul's encounter with the island people of Malta, we found the principle that God supplies the supernatural power to do what He directs us to do. Paul had seen the Lord work miracles before, and by faith he prayed boldly for healing.

God may or may not be leading you to prayers of healing, but He often directs us to action that will require faith in His supernatural power to accomplish.

Take a moment to reflect and identify one area where you need God's supernatural power today:

Perhaps you desire to see real changes in your habits when it comes to your prayer life. Others of you might need patience to wait on God's timing. Some of you sense God directing you to take a risk, make a big move, or pursue new opportunities. Even if you feel like you've just come out of a metaphorical ship-wreck in your life, the Lord wants to infuse you with His supernatural power for the work ahead.

Write a simple prayer below inviting the Holy Spirit to direct and fill you with God's power:

Even while documenting the snakebite and healings, Luke doesn't record any details of conversions. We can assume that Paul likely shared the gospel with the natives on Malta, but we don't know if any of them believed in Jesus or not.[18] Paul helped and healed people even when they didn't respond to Christ's invitation. He was persuasive without being punitive. Paul would need this posture as he later faced rejection from many Jewish leaders in Rome.

Extra Insights

"Malta…on which the ship was wrecked, is an island about 18 miles long and 8 miles wide."[14] It is about 58 miles south of Sicily. The most commonly held assumption is that the shipwreck landed at St. Paul's Bay, which is about 3 to 4 miles from the northeast tip of the island.[15]

"Malta lacks poisonous snakes today, so some scholars suggest here the nontoxic *Coronella austriaca*, which resembles a viper and can act as in 28:3-4."[16] Since the natives expected Paul to die, it's likely that they had some experience with poisonous snakes in ancient times, even though Malta has no venomous snakes in their modern ecology.[17]

Extra Insights

Read Acts 28:11-31 and answer the following questions:

Commentators' speculations about the cause of Publius's father's fever vary. Some cite malaria since the Greek word used for fever is plural and malarial fevers can be intermittent. Others believe it was the "Malta fever" that comes from a microorganism found in the milk of Malta's goats, which can also be "recurrent and persistent." Still others object that dysentery isn't linked with either of those maladies and might be food poisoning or infected water.[19]

Where did Paul finally arrive? (v. 14)

What did Paul do just three days after his arrival in Rome? (v. 17)

Why did he call them? (v. 20)

What was the only thing the Jewish leaders in Rome knew about the Christian movement? (v. 22)

What did Paul use to explain and try to persuade the Jews about the kingdom of God? (v. 23)

What was the outcome of Paul's speaking from morning until evening? (v. 24)

Who did Paul say would accept God's salvation? (v. 28)

What did Paul do during the next two years in Rome? (v. 31)

The Alexandrian ship bearing the twin gods (Acts 28:11) represented the sons of Zeus named Castor and Pollux. They were considered "patrons of navigation, and their constellation (Gemini) was a sign of good fortune when seen in a storm."[20]

The believers in Rome encouraged Paul and caused him to thank God. After planting so many seeds of faith, Paul must have found great joy in seeing them grow—even in cities where he hadn't directly been involved. The group of travelers took a famous Roman road referred to as the Appian Way and traveled 125 miles on toward Rome from their ship's final landing port in Puteoli. When they were about forty-three miles from Rome, the first group of Christians met with Paul. When they were ten miles from Rome, another group of believers visited him at the Three Taverns.[21]

Once he arrived in Rome, Paul didn't waste time in calling for the Jewish leaders. Likely Paul wanted to know if they had received any communication regarding the charges against him from the leaders in Jerusalem who had plotted to kill him.

Soon after making his defense, Paul took an opportunity to share the message of Christ with the people from his own upbringing and culture. Some commentators estimate that there would have been twenty thousand to thirty thousand Jews who worshipped in several different synagogues throughout the city.[23] While Paul is called the apostle to the Gentiles, he never missed an opportunity to present the truth about Jesus to his fellow Jews living in other cities (Acts 14:1; 17:1, 10, 17; 18:4; 19:8; 28:17).

Some believed his message, but the majority rejected it. Paul quoted the prophet Isaiah regarding his own people's hard hearts, deaf ears, and blind eyes. Perhaps he hoped to provoke these Jews not to make the same mistakes of the leaders in Jerusalem, who had called for the crucifixion of the Messiah sent from God. He wanted the Jews in Rome to see that Jesus had the power to save them.

Paul faithfully proclaimed the message, but he left the results in God's hands. It must have been heartbreaking to see his Jewish brothers and sisters, who had anticipated the Messiah's coming for generations, close their ears to the message, yet he had learned to shake off the dust and go to the Gentiles (Luke 10:10-11).

Throughout Acts we've found not only the birth but also the expansion of the church. Even in chains, Paul met with fellow believers for mutual encouragement. And from him we can learn not to measure our spiritual lives by fruitfulness but by faithfulness.

My husband recently reminded me that an apple seed planted in the ground won't see a single piece of fruit for six to ten years. As we share with others from the Scriptures and from our own spiritual stories, we can call on what we've learned from Paul—that we should not get too caught up in outcomes. God will bring the fruit while we focus on faithfully spreading the seeds.

Think about some ways you might spread seeds of faith in the coming week. Consider these ideas or add a different one of your own and put a star by one you will act upon:

- **Call a friend and tell them your key takeaways from studying Acts.**

- **Show up in person to show someone you care. (The believers in Rome encouraged Paul with their presence.)**

- **Send a card, text, email, or other message to let someone know you are thinking of them or praying for them.**

- **Meet a physical/financial need and tell the recipient that God loves them and sees them.**

- **Share your personal story of faith with someone else.**

"During these two years in Rome, Paul wrote Philippians, Ephesians, Colossians, and Philemon....He had Timothy with him (Phil. 1:1; 2:19; Col. 1:1), as well as John Mark, Luke, Aristarchus, Epaphras, Justus, and Demas (Col. 4:10-14; Philem. 24). He also met Philemon's runaway slave, Onesimus, and led him to faith in Christ (Philem. 10–21)."[22]

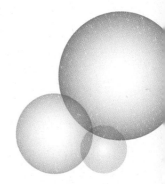

God directed Paul, and He wants to lead us. We may not be traveling missionaries, church planters, or preachers, but the Lord wants us to be faithful in our callings.

Daily Wrap-Up

What is one way you noticed God at work in Acts 28?

How did the believers respond?

God protected Paul from a snakebite and enabled him to heal many people on the island of Malta. The Lord also encouraged Paul through the presence of other believers and used him to present the gospel message to the Jewish leaders. Paul allowed himself to be God's instrument and boldly proclaimed that Jesus was the Messiah.

Through Paul's example in Acts 28, we learned that:

- God supplies the supernatural power we need for anything He directs us to do.
- Outcomes are in God's hands.

We can focus on faithfulness, knowing that God will supply the power we need to serve Him. As we let this truth sink deep, we can attempt more God-sized tasks with confidence. We don't have to measure the results—those are up to the Lord. Instead, we plant seeds that others may water, trusting God to bring growth.

Today we focused on this truth: *God calls us to faithfulness so that He can bring greater fruitfulness.*

How would you summarize your personal takeaway from today's lesson?

Sharing my faith with two people seemed impossible to me on that first day of college, but the Lord gave me an opportunity on an airplane and in a conversation with several people in a park. Talking about God can seem overwhelming, but when I remember that I don't have to do it in my own strength, it takes the pressure off. The Lord will supernaturally give us the power to do anything He directs us to do.

Talk with God

Lord, I want to get out of my comfort zone as You lead me. Talking to other people about You seems scary at times. Help me to listen for Your direction and depend on You for the words and timing. Sometimes I get so caught up with this life that I forget about heaven. Lord, give me boldness to share with others so they have the opportunity to know Your love and grace. Amen.

Memory Verse Exercise

Read the Memory Verse on page 170 several times, and then fill in the blanks below as you recite it:

_____ I will _____ you from _____ _____ own
_____ and the _____. Yes, I am _____
you to the _____ to _____ their _____, so they
may _____ from _____ to _____ and from the
_____ of _____ to God. _____ they will _____
_____ for their _____ and be _____ a
place _____ God's _____, who are _____ _____ by
_____ in me.

(Acts 26:17-18)

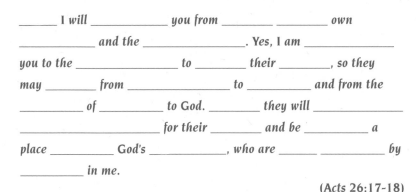

Day 5: Unstoppable Directions

I often listen to true crime stories either through podcasts or television shows. My husband and I were looking through our viewing options recently, and he suggested a series about unsolved mysteries. He was deferring to my tastes, and I was engaged in the first episode until I realized that the cases ended without resolution. When the episode finished, the watcher was left with many questions and no conclusions.

We decided not to keep watching when I discovered the missing element of justice toward the offender. My husband and I watch television for relaxation and entertainment. I didn't want to leave the experience without answers because it left me unsettled.

I wonder if any of you finished the Book of Acts yesterday feeling like it ended abruptly. I found myself wondering what happened to Paul after the two years spent in Rome. Commentators have wrestled with the time line, speculating

Scripture Focus

Acts 1:8

Big Idea

Awakening spiritually gives us eyes to see and ears to hear the unstoppable work of God in drawing all people to Himself.

whether Luke knew about Paul's death at the time he wrote Acts. One scholar pointed out that "abrupt endings were...fairly common in ancient literature, and did not mean that the writer did not know some events that followed."[25] Here were some of the possibilities to what may have happened after Paul's two years in Rome, according to Greek scholar I. Howard Marshall:

- At Luke's writing of Acts, he didn't know what happened after the two years in Rome.
- The Jews from Jerusalem could have failed to appear in order to prosecute the case, and Paul would have been automatically released after the appropriate time had lapsed.
- Paul could have been tried and then released, or the case dropped by the Romans.
- Paul may have been tried and executed, but Luke didn't want to record his martyrdom.[26]

What we do know is that eventually, hundreds or even thousands of Christians were hunted and killed in Rome under Nero. If Paul was released after the two years, he was then rearrested later and martyred.[27]

While our human desire for closure on Paul's life might leave us wanting at the end of Acts, we know that Luke accomplished his task of recording the spread of the gospel. He wasn't chronicling the story of individuals but the movement of God.

In the Book of Acts, we watched the church grow from a small group of Christ-followers to a widespread movement. We can go back to Acts 1:8 and see how it unfolded. Jesus told His disciples, "But you will receive power when the Holy Spirit comes upon you. And you will be my witnesses, telling people about me everywhere—in Jerusalem, throughout Judea, in Samaria, and to the ends of the earth" (Acts 1:8).

God's unstoppable plan went forward. Some hearers of God's message chose to believe and awaken to God in their everyday lives, and others continued on their own paths.

Read just a few of the ways Jesus's words in Acts 1:8 came to fruition:

Place	Witness	Verses	Situation
Jerusalem	Peter	Acts 2:14	Peter preached in Jerusalem on the Day of Pentecost.
Judea	All believers except the apostles	Acts 8:1	A great wave of persecution of the church in Jerusalem forced the believers to scatter throughout the region of Judea and Samaria.
Samaria	Philip	Acts 8:5	Philip preached and cast out evil spirits in Samaria after the persecution scattered the believers away from Jerusalem.
The Ends of the Earth	Paul	Acts 13–21	Paul and many companion disciples took three missionary journeys spreading the gospel message far and wide.

The Lord accomplished what He set out to do in growing the church from Jerusalem, Judea, Samaria, and to the ends of the earth. In the centuries since, His message reached you and me. His unstoppable plan advanced even though men like Nero tried to extinguish the Christian faith. As we look back on the gospel movement throughout Acts, we've seen these two truths highlighted:

- God can and will accomplish His purposes.
- God chooses to use people who will believe Him and become His instruments.

Before we take some time to review what we've learned, I want to share the closing remarks of the commentators who have helped to provide our background information for Acts along the way:

> "You and I live in the continuation of the story of Acts. Acts must close in an open-ended fashion, with the door still open for work and witness rather than closed by death, because the Spirit is still active. Luke is not simply writing history. He writes the story of the Spirit, the Spirit incarnate in people like you and me."[28]

> "The kingdom is God's doing, and whatever the obstacles and apparent setbacks along the way, God steadily advances it."[29]

> "Luke did not write his book simply to record ancient history. He wrote to encourage the church in every age to be faithful to the Lord and carry the gospel to the ends of the earth."[30]

Though these commentators didn't agree on every bit of history and theology in their approaches to Acts, they all agreed that the abrupt ending serves to help remind us that we are part of this story.

Which one of these statements resonated most with you and why?

God's mission will move forward just as surely as the sun will rise each day. We have to decide whether we will get up and join His work as faithful witnesses or push the spiritual snooze button.

Let's take some time to thoughtfully review what we've learned over the course of the last six sessions. Read through the key areas of emphasis and record a brief answer to each reflection question. (If this is overwhelming, pick two or three questions to answer.)

Week	Reflection Question	Your Brief Answer
Awakening to God's Power (Acts 1–4)	What have you learned or experienced about the power of God's Holy Spirit?	
Awakening to God's Message (Acts 5–9)	How would you summarize in your own words the gospel message shared in a variety of different ways by different people in Acts?	
Awakening to God's Freedom (Acts 10–14)	How does the early church's journey to freedom from favoritism, tradition, and/or bondage inspire you toward spiritual freedom in your own life?	
Awakening to God's Grace (Acts 15–19)	Where is the Lord currently calling you to keep an open mind, listen earnestly, and search the Scriptures like the Bereans we read about in Acts 17?	
Awakening to God's Mission (Acts 20–24)	Where do you currently sense the Lord calling you to serve Him and share your life with others?	
Awakening to God's Direction (Acts 25–28)	How does Paul's journey inspire you to either wait or move forward in an area where you are seeking God's direction?	

As you reflect on the weeks of study, write one or two key takeaways for you personally from the Book of Acts:

Each day in our study, we asked what God was doing and how believers responded to His work. Some days we witnessed God's divine intervention, and other chapters revealed Him working behind the scenes. The believers responded in a variety of ways, including gathering, teaching, praying, praising, displaying generosity, serving one another, and many other spiritual practices. The thirty years we covered in our study of Acts changed the world forever. God's unstoppable plan went forth, and it continues with forward motion today.

One day Jesus will return for the church that was established in Acts. The people have changed, but the message and mission remain the same. Until He comes, we can grow in faith and be used as His instruments to share His gospel through the power of the Holy Spirit. I pray that as you finished Acts, you were inspired to see God at work and ask how you might awaken to God more and more in your everyday life.

Talk with God

God, I am amazed by all that I have studied in Acts. Reading your unstoppable plans for the early church reminds me that You are still at work today. Open my eyes and ears to see how I can be more aware of Your kingdom here on earth. Awaken my soul to know You more and more. Give me Holy Spirit power to seek Your direction for my life each day.

Memory Verse Exercise

Read the Memory Verse on page 170 several times, and then fill in the blanks below as you recite it:

_____ I _____ _____ *you from* _____ _____ *own*
_____ *and the* _____. _____, *I am* _____
_____ *to the* _____ *to* _____ *their* _____, *so*
_____ *may* _____ *from* _____ *to* _____
and _____ *the* _____ *of* _____ *to* _____. _____
they will _____ _____ _____ *for* _____
_____ *and be* _____ *a* _____ _____ _____
_____, *who are* _____ _____ *by* _____ *in me.*
                                                    (Acts 26:17-18)

Video Viewer Guide: Week 6

Acts 25:6-12

God's direction doesn't dictate a _____ position.

How have you taught others how to _____ you?

Acts 27:21-26

God's direction doesn't decree _____ _____ circumstances.

God's directions are typically more _____ than _____.

Acts 28:30

God is still at work awakening us to:

- God's _____

- God's _____

- God's _____

- God's _____

- God's _____

- God's _____

Notes

Week 1

1. William H. Willimon, *Acts*, Interpretation (Louisville: Westminster John Knox, 1988, repr. 2010), 8.
2. Willimon, *Acts*, 2.
3. Merrill C. Tenney and Richard N. Longenecker, *John–Acts*, vol. 9 of *The Expositor's Bible* Commentary, ed. Frank E. Gaebelein (Grand Rapids, MI: Zondervan, 1981), 217.
4. Tenney and Longenecker, *John–Acts*, 238.
5. Warren W. Wiersbe, *Be Dynamic: Experience the Power of God's People*, NT Commentary: Acts 1–12 (Colorado Springs, CO: David C. Cook), 20.
6. I. Howard Marshall, *Acts: An Introduction and Commentary* (Nottingham: InterVarsity Press, 1980), 60.
7. *The NAS New Testament Greek Lexicon*, s.v. "Baptizo," https://www.biblestudytools.com/lexicons/greek/nas/baptizo.html.
8. Tenney and Longenecker, *John–Acts*, 256.
9. Craig S. Keener, *Acts* (Cambridge: Cambridge University Press, 2020), 70–71.
10. Willimon, *Acts*, 22–23.
11. Keener, *Acts*, 131.
12. Tenney and Longenecker, *John–Acts*, 269.
13. Tenney and Longenecker, *John–Acts*, 270.
14. *The NAS New Testament Greek Lexicon*, s.v. "Lambano," https://www.biblestudytools.com/lexicons/greek/nas/lambano.html.
15. Tenney and Longenecker, *John–Acts*, 293.
16. Keener, *Acts*, 185.
17. Merrill F. Unger, *The New Unger's Bible Dictionary*, ed. R. K. Harrison, rev. and updated edition (Chicago: Moody Press, 1988), 1045.
18. Tenney and Longenecker, *John–Acts*, 294.
19. Marshall, *Acts*, 104.
20. Marshall, *Acts*, 110.
21. Wiersbe, *Be Dynamic*, 68.
22. Wiersbe, *Be Dynamic*, 61.

Week 2

1. Tenney and Longenecker, *John–Acts*, 315.
2. Wiersbe, *Be Dynamic*, 104.
3. Keener, *Acts*, 225.
4. Keener, *Acts*, 221.

5. Keener, *Acts*, 103.
6. Wiersbe, *Be Dynamic*, 103.
7. Keener, *Acts*, 233.
8. Marshall, *Acts*, 142–43.
9. Marshall, *Acts*, 144.
10. Marshall, *Acts*, 157.
11. Unger, *The New Unger's Bible Dictionary*, 1117.
12. Marshall, *Acts*, 167.
13. Marshall, *Acts*, 172.
14. Marshall, *Acts*, 174.
15. Marshall, *Acts*, 171.
16. Willimon, *Acts*, 77.
17. Willimon, *Acts*, 78–79.
18. Willimon, *Acts*, 76–77.

Week 3

1. Keener, *Acts*, 295.
2. Tenney and Longenecker, *John–Acts*, 387.
3. Keener, *Acts*, 297.
4. Tenney and Longenecker, *John–Acts*, 383.
5. Keener, *Acts*, 300.
6. Keener, *Acts*, 301.
7. Tenney and Longenecker, *John–Acts*, 390.
8. Wiersbe, *Be Dynamic*, 149.
9. Keener, *Acts*, 300.
10. Marshall, *Acts*, 203.
11. Marshall, *Acts*, 203.
12. Marshall, *Acts*, 216.
13. Keener, *Acts*, 20.
14. Marshall, *Acts*, 225.
15. Keener, *Acts*, 334.
16. Keener, *Acts*, 335.
17. Marshall, *Acts*, 236.
18. *The KJV New Testament Greek Lexicon*, s.v. "Chara," https://www.biblestudytools.com/lexicons/greek/kjv/chara.html.
19. *The KJV New Testament Greek Lexicon*, s.v. "Charis," https://www.biblestudytools.com/lexicons/greek/kjv/charis.html.
20. "Why Multitasking Doesn't Work," Health Essentials, Cleveland Clinic, March 10, 2021, https://health.clevelandclinic.org/science-clear-multitasking-doesnt-work/Science.
21. Tenney and Longenecker, *John–Acts*, 438.
22. Tenney and Longenecker, *John–Acts*, 433.
23. Keener, *Acts*, 349.

24. Keener, *Acts*, 350.

25. Tenney and Longenecker, *John–Acts*, 435.

26. Tenney and Longenecker, *John–Acts*, 436.

Week 4

1. Unger, *The New Unger's Bible Dictionary*, 238.

2. Tenney and Longenecker, *John–Acts*, 444.

3. Keener, *Acts*, 359.

4. Tenney and Longenecker, *John–Acts*, 445.

5. Warren W. Wiersbe, *Be Daring* (Colorado Springs: David C Cook, 1988), 33.

6. Keener, *Acts*, 361.

7. Wiersbe, *Be Daring*, 42.

8. Oxford English Dictionary, s.v. "deference," https://www.lexico.com/en/definition/deference.

9. Marshall, *Acts*, 277.

10. Marshall, *Acts*, 279.

11. Marshall, *Acts*, 282.

12. Ralph Gower, *The New Manners and Customs of Bible Times* (Chicago: Moody Press, 1987), 282.

13. Wiersbe, *Be Daring*, 54.

14. Tenney and Longenecker, *John–Acts*, 468.

15. *The NAS New Testament Greek Lexicon*, s.v. "dialegomai," https://www.biblestudytools.com/lexicons/greek/nas/dialegomai.html.

16. Wiersbe, *Be Daring*, 54.

17. Keener, *Acts*, 426.

18. Tenney and Longenecker, *John–Acts*, 473.

19. Tenney and Longenecker, *John–Acts*, 480.

20. Keener, *Acts*, 452.

21. Tenney and Longenecker, *John–Acts*, 481.

22. Wiersbe, *Be Daring*, 68.

23. Marshall, *Acts*, 327.

24. Marshall, *Acts*, 329.

25. Tenney and Longenecker, *John–Acts*, 493.

26. Willimon, *Acts*, 152; Marshall, *Acts*, 335.

Week 5

1. *The NAS New Testament Greek Lexicon*, s.v. "Matheteuo," https://www.biblestudytools.com/lexicons/greek/nas/matheteuo.html.

2. Tenney and Longenecker, *John–Acts*, 507.

3. Willimon, *Acts*, 153.

4. Wiersbe, *Be Daring*, 96.

5. Marshall, *Acts*, 345.

6. Marshall, *Acts*, 358–59.

7. Wiersbe, *Be Daring*, 111.
8. Keener, *Acts*, 513.
9. Marshall, *Acts*, 359; Keener, *Acts*, 514.
10. Keener, *Acts*, 521.
11. Marshall, *Acts*, 367.
12. Wiersbe, *Be Daring*, 115.
13. Marshall, *Acts*, 364.
14. Keener, *Acts*, 525–26.
15. Keener, *Acts*, 537.
16. Tenney and Longenecker, *John–Acts*, 524–25.
17. Keener, *Acts*, 531.
18. Tenney and Longenecker, *John–Acts*, 528.
19. Keener, *Acts*, 542.
20. Marshall, *Acts*, 378; see also Keener, *Acts*, 541.
21. Tenney and Longenecker, *John–Acts*, 530.
22. Marshall, *Acts*, 382; Wiersbe, *Be Daring*, 126.
23. Tenney and Longenecker, *John–Acts*, 531.
24. Marshall, *Acts*, 384; Keener, *Acts*, 546.
25. Wiersbe, *Be Daring*, 124.
26. Marshall, *Acts*, 389; see also Keener, *Acts*, 552.
27. Keener, *Acts*, 568.
28. Wiersbe, *Be Daring*, 143.
29. Marshall, *Acts*, 393.
30. Keener, *Acts*, 556.
31. Tenney and Longenecker, *John–Acts*, 543.

Week 6

1. Keener, *Acts*, 575; Tenney and Longenecker, *John–Acts*, 546.
2. Keener, *Acts*, 578.
3. Keener, *Acts*, 580.
4. Tenney and Longenecker, *John–Acts*, 552.
5. Wiersbe, *Be Daring*, 156.
6. Marshall, *Acts*, 419.
7. Keener, *Acts*, 592.
8. Wiersbe, *Be Daring*, 165.
9. Tenney and Longenecker, *John–Acts*, 558.
10. Keener, *Acts*, 595–96.
11. *The NAS New Testament Greek Lexicon*, s.v. "parrhesiazomai," biblestudytools .com/lexicons/Greek/nas/parrhesiazomai.html.
12. Tenney and Longenecker, *John–Acts*, 560; see also, Marshall, *Acts*, 428.
13. Keener, *Acts*, 22.
14. Tenney and Longenecker, *John–Acts*, 563.
15. Keener, *Acts*, 611.

16. Keener, *Acts*, 613.
17. Tenney and Longenecker, *John–Acts*, 564.
18. Marshall, *Acts*, 438.
19. Keener, *Acts*, 616; see also, Tenney and Longenecker, *John–Acts*, 565.
20. Marshall, *Acts*, 439.
21. Wiersbe, *Be Daring*, 171.
22. Wiersbe, *Be Daring*, 172–73.
23. Keener, *Acts*, 624–25.
24. Tenney and Longenecker, *John–Acts*, 572.
25. Keener, *Acts*, 46.
26. Marshall, *Acts*, 446–47.
27. Keener, *Acts*, 632.
28. Willimon, *Acts*, 192.
29. Keener, *Acts*, 634.
30. Wiersbe, *Be Daring*, 174.

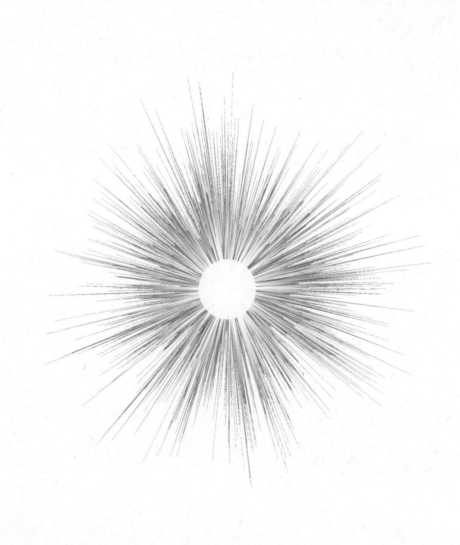

The Roman Road

The Roman Empire was known for its system of roads that were efficient, well-patrolled, and built to last. They helped travelers navigate their journeys with mile markers and well-designed paths. The saying "All roads lead to Rome" came about as a result of the meticulous planning and engineering of Roman roadways that came out of the capital city.

However, the Christian reference to "The Roman Road" is more about spiritual pathways than physical ones. The Roman Road is a term used for taking some key verses from the Book of Romans to explain the way in which a person becomes a Christian.

We need a word of caution, however, when it comes to using a tool like The Roman Road. It really isn't a road but instead some of the key pavers. Studying verses in context and with historical background give us a more complete picture of what it means to be a Christ-follower. Salvation is much more than a past experience where we read a few verses from Romans and pray a prayer so that we will go to heaven when we die.

Following Jesus is as much a present reality as it is a past experience. So as we look at these verses from Romans that frame a gospel road map of sorts, let's keep in mind that these truths are a starting point. The journey in a relationship with Christ is filled with crossroads, stop signs, hills, and valleys. Sometimes we even go off-roading at times, following our own ways. Then we get back on the path and seek God again.

Yet again, those whose study of Romans has them asking good questions like:

What does it look like to begin a relationship with God?
How could I explain the good news about Jesus to someone?
Can I be sure that I will go to heaven when I die?

The Roman Road can be a helpful tool in understanding the key stepping-stones toward a relationship with Jesus. People have used different verses in a variety of orders but most include these pavers:

God made us and loves us. By faith we believe that God created the world and loves His creation.

"For ever since the world was created, people have seen the earth and sky. Through everything God made, they can clearly see his invisible qualities—his eternal power and divine nature. So they have no excuse for not knowing God."

(Romans 1:20)

"No power in the sky above or in the earth below—indeed, nothing in all creation will ever be able to separate us from the love of God that is revealed in Christ Jesus our Lord."

(Romans 8:39)

Sin messed everything up. By faith we believe that sin brings spiritual death and separation from a holy God.

"As the Scriptures say, 'No one is righteous—not even one.'"

(Romans 3:10)

"For everyone has sinned; we all fall short of God's glorious standard."

(Romans 3:23)

Christ paid the penalty for our sin. By faith we believe that Christ was the perfect sacrifice to cleanse us from sin and restore our relationship with God.

"But God showed his great love for us by sending Christ to die for us while we were still sinners."

(Romans 5:8)

"For the wages of sin is death, but the free gift of God is eternal life through Christ Jesus our Lord."

(Romans 6:23)

We personally believe and receive grace by faith. By faith we start a relationship with God by saying and believing that Jesus is the way to God.

"If you openly declare that Jesus is Lord and believe in your heart that God raised him from the dead, you will be saved. For it is by believing in your heart that you are made right with God, and it is by openly declaring your faith that you are saved."

(Romans 10:9-10)

"For 'Everyone who calls on the name of the LORD will be saved.'"

(Romans 10:13)

Remember that the good news that changes everything is about faith from start to finish (Romans 1:17). We don't need to "do" something spiritual or pray a "proper" salvation prayer. Instead, we believe by faith that what God says is true. We take spiritual steps down our own journeys and seek to connect with the God of the universe who is crazy about us and sent His Son to die for us.

Video Viewer Guide Answers

Introductory Video

physically / spiritually

social media, television, material possessions

prayer, Bible study, worship, journaling, silence

tasks / relationships

telling others the Good News about the wonderful grace of God

birthed / sustains

Week 1

passion for God / God's Power

information / transformation

very presence of God

prayer

fix

action

Week 2

God's Message / mess

mess / age

God's Message / service

God's Message / communicate it clearly

partnership / full ownership

Week 3

law / letter / spirit

Jesus / religion

one thing / another

want / need

push back / freedom steps

Week 4

grace / others / we

disagreements

face, face / listen / ask questions / Scriptures

Exit

Week 5

overwhelming / apathetic

faithfulness

dependency

humility

Week 6

doormat

treat

Disney World

daily / distant

power / message / freedom / grace / mission / direction

Stream videos wherever you meet— together or at home.

Call **800-672-1789** for the latest offer.
All subscriptions begin with a **free 14-day trial**.

Amplify Media is a multimedia platform that delivers high quality, searchable content for church-wide, group, or individual use on any device at any time. In a world of sometimes overwhelming choices, Amplify gives church leaders media capabilities that are contemporary, relevant, effective and, most importantly, affordable and sustainable.

With Amplify Media you can:

- provide a reliable source of Christian content for teaching, training, and inspiration in a customizable library;
- deliver your own preaching and worship content in a way your congregation knows and appreciates;
- build your church's capacity to innovate with engaging content and accessible technology;
- equip your congregation to better understand the Bible and its application; and
- deepen discipleship beyond the church walls.

Sign up for Amplify Media at:
https://www.amplifymedia.com/pricing.